Head Start

Pearson

At Pearson, we have a simple mission: to help people make more of their lives through learning.

We combine innovative learning technology with trusted content and educational expertise to provide engaging and effective learning experiences that serve people wherever and whenever they are learning.

From classroom to boardroom, our curriculum materials, digital learning tools and testing programmes help to educate millions of people worldwide – more than any other private enterprise.

Every day our work helps learning flourish, and wherever learning flourishes, so do people.

To learn more, please visit us at **www.pearson.com/uk**

Head Start

Build a resilient mindset and achieve your goals

Ian Price

 Pearson

Harlow, England • London • New York • Boston • San Francisco • Toronto • Sydney
Dubai • Singapore • Hong Kong • Tokyo • Seoul • Taipei • New Delhi
Cape Town • São Paulo • Mexico City • Madrid • Amsterdam • Munich • Paris • Milan

PEARSON EDUCATION LIMITED
KAO Two
KAO Park
Harlow
CM17 9NA
United Kingdom
Tel: +44 (0)1279 623623
Web: www.pearson.com/uk

First edition published 2018 (print and electronic)

© Pearson Education Limited 2018 (print and electronic)

ISBN: 978-1-292-24380-1 (print)
       978-1-292-24381-8 (PDF)
       978-1-292-24382-5 (ePub)

British Library Cataloguing-in-Publication Data
A catalogue record for the print edition is available from the British Library

Library of Congress Cataloging-in-Publication Data
A catalog record for the print edition is available from the Library of Congress

10 9 8 7 6 5 4 3 2 1

22 21 20 19 18

Cover design by Two Associates
Cover and spine image © OSTILL/iStock/Getty Images Plus/Getty Images

Print edition typeset in 9.5/13pt Mundo Sans Pro by Pearson CSC
Printed by Ashford Colour Press Ltd, Gosport

NOTE THAT ANY PAGE CROSS REFERENCES REFER TO THE PRINT EDITION

In memory of Reed Morgan (1964–2018)

Contents

Chapter 10   The virtuous habits of high
            performance

About the author

Ian is a performance psychologist who helps organisations and leaders achieve their goals by building their resilience and mental toughness.

His first degree was in English Literature at Magdalen College, University of Oxford, where he learned some early lessons in resilience en route to gaining a Half Blue in boxing. He began his career at strategy consultants LEK before moving into the telecoms industry, holding a number of senior positions in companies including BT Group.

Photo by Jai Shah Photography
(jai@jaishah.co.uk)

Always curious about psychology, he changed career in 2008 and began a two-year MSc in Organisational Behaviour at Birkbeck, University of London. He has practised as an independent business psychologist since 2010 and is a member of the Association of Business Psychologists. His consulting company counts Worldpay, ei Group (formerly Enterprise Inns), Deloitte Digital and Punter Southall Group among its clients.

More information can be found at www.headstartprogramme.co.uk

Ian lives in London and is married to Iyabo, who puts his resilience to the test most weeks when she plays him at tennis. They have one son, Alex.

Acknowledgements

In putting this book together, I am indebted to a number of people for their guidance and support along the way. Among psychologists I'd like to single out Rob Archer and Merlin Van de Braam. Among writers, I'd like to thank Paul Morland and Julian Costley. A number of people at Pearson have given me tireless support and I'd like to single out Eloise Cook, Antje King, Priya Dhanagopal, Chimaechi Allan, Mary Lince and Suzanne Pattinson for their superb work along with the rest of the team. Finally, my thanks to my wife Iyabo for her support and counsel.

Introduction

'Twenty years from now you'll be more disappointed by the things you didn't do than the things you did do. So throw off the bowlines. Sail away from the safe harbour.'

Attributed to Mark Twain

What's the secret of achieving our goals? How can we become resilient enough to get there?

Are there any desires or ambitions in your work or life that fit into the 'I've always wanted to...' category? Or are there specific milestones that you'd like to hit in your career? If so, what has stopped you achieving them before now?

This may be to do with negative beliefs:

- I could never do that.
- I'm not good enough.
- I don't have the motivation – I'm too lazy.
- I don't have the time, what with work and family.
- I'm too old.
- If it were going to happen, it would have happened by now.
- I'm not confident enough.

Or, alternatively, it may be more to do with negative behaviours:

- I give up – I quit.
- I don't persist.
- I procrastinate.
- I let myself get distracted.

If any of these negative beliefs and behaviours strike a chord, then you are not alone. If you'd like to change them, then this is where Head Start comes in.

It turns out that the equipment to succeed is something you already have – your mind. Not only that, it also turns out that whatever aspect of mindset is obstructing you in your achievement of your goals, behavioural scientists have made enormous headway in recent years in their understanding of why it is so often a barrier and, more importantly, have come up with tools to help us change it and build our abilities.

This book will:

1. Help you reframe your negative beliefs.

2. Provide you with science-based tools to change your behaviour.

3. Give you a further toolkit of best practice habits to help you on your way.

The figure below shows this graphically.

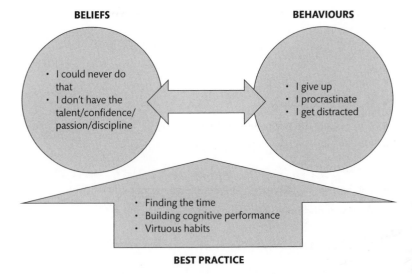

For further resources go to www.headstartbook.com

Why we need resilience

Some of us are beaten by the setbacks and challenges that life inevitably scatters across our path. If we lack resilience and the ability to bounce back, we are likely to simply to give up. For others, the fear of failure or lack of confidence can cause us to retreat into our comfort zone and avoid risk. This means we don't even try in the first place. Or it may be that our day job leaves us with too little time or energy to pursue our dreams.

In short, we just never get started and reconcile ourselves to disappointment. This can mean that we miss out on pursuing activities that might be enjoyable and fulfilling. In work, this can lead to demotivation and disengagement.

Of course, external factors certainly play a part. A lucky break can send you on your way while a reversal can knock you on your backside. There is only so much you can do to influence these factors. What you can influence, however, is your mental reaction to them.

Most of what lies within our control is to do with our mindset. And our mindset in turn drives our beliefs and our behaviours. This book will help you build a resilient mindset so that you can confront the fear of failure, venture outside your comfort zone and learn to persist in the face of adversity.

No matter how positive our mindset, no matter how great our motivation, success is ultimately driven by what we do. This is particularly the case when things get tough, such as when we encounter setbacks or reach a plateau.

So what behaviours do we exhibit when we try to achieve our goals? Do we start with good intentions but then get distracted by other things such as TV or social media? Do we take to heart unhelpful criticism from others and simply give up?

Success in achieving our goals is determined by the interplay between our beliefs and our behaviours. This book will work on both and will provide you with a science-based structure for your detailed goal-setting. As we go through each chapter you will build a personalised development plan for building the right mindset for goal achievement.

The importance of mindset

When we see others succeeding, it's easy to explain that away as a function of talent or simply luck. How do we know that mindset plays a part?

Olympic athletes and the gold standard of success

For an example, let's take something recent and familiar – Britain's perform-ance in the 2016 Olympics at Rio.

In 1996, Britain's team of athletes returned from the Olympic Games in Atlanta with one solitary gold medal in rowing. This was a low point in British international sporting achievement and was the subject of a good deal of national self-flagellation in the media. Fast-forward to 2016 and Team GB built on the success of London 2012 with an even greater haul of medals.

In case people attributed the success of London 2012 to the fact that Brit-ain was hosting the games, Britain's performance at Rio in 2016 made it the first host nation to actually increase its tally of medals.

The scale of this achievement is astonishing. In 20 years Britain went from one solitary gold and being 32nd in the medals table to 27 golds and sec-ond in the table to the US. To what is this success attributable?

In the narrative that has taken hold, the answer to that question usually revolves around Sir John Major, the National Lottery and the hundreds of millions of pounds invested in elite sport. But, as is often the case with narrative, this explanation is too simple.

The money has, of course, made an enormous impact, particularly in pro-viding the means for promising athletes to dedicate themselves full-time to training. But this increase in investment as an explanation for Olympic success is too simplistic. After all, examples abound in sport, particularly in football, of vast amounts of money being spent with no demonstrable success.

In addition to the influx of money, there was a change of mindset in UK sport. The discipline and science-based approach perfected in those sports, such as rowing (where Britain had achieved Olympic success), were applied elsewhere. This meant that sports in Britain, for those sports deemed to have serious chances of winning medals, benefited from a professional approach that was unprecedented. As well as coaching in skills and techniques, athletes were benefiting from the application of science and the latest thinking in nutrition.

UK Sport performance director Simon Timson called this approach 'Success by design'.

What if a similar transformation were available today for the rest of us? Is there a leap in capability comparable to that experienced by British Olympians from the dark days of the late twentieth century? Can we take a 'success by design' approach to our own ambitions in work and life?

The good news is that you can bring about an equally dramatic change in your own mindset. If you decide to take control of your own personal development, then the contents of this book will help you plan and achieve a similar transformation to the one pulled off by British sport.

From sporting glory to the workplace

So how is it possible to bottle the Olympic effect for us ordinary mortals? Businesses often attempt to transfer examples of sporting glory to the workplace but with limited results. The similarities between sport and business are frequently observed and successful sports personalities are well-represented as speakers at conferences.

A motivational talk from a former world champion is almost always entertaining and can be inspiring in a transient way, providing a brief uplift of positivity. But this only acts as a sugar pill and the feeling is almost entirely lost on return to the office. Why? Because tales of last-minute tries or trans-Atlantic sailing heroics are not obviously transferrable to the workplace.

As economist Jeremy Warner wrote in *The Daily Telegraph* during the Rio Olympics: 'Too much is often made of the apparent parallels between business and sports success. Victory on the track is not going to make you into a successful entrepreneur, or even corporate executive.'[1]

This is because athletic success is often determined by physical ability: strength, speed, hand-eye co-ordination. Business people succeed through their wits or, in psychologists' language, their cognitive performance. Likewise, we shall see that success outside work is driven by attitude and mindset much more than by any innate ability. This concept of cognitive performance is what we are going to focus on in this book.

Because what is transferrable from gold-winning Olympians is the science-based approach to building cognitive performance. It is this that has in recent years transformed a number of sports. As has increasingly been observed, once the physical aspects of training and skills development have been mastered by athletes, achievement on the day is mostly about mental performance. During the Rio Olympics in August 2016, sports psychologist Amanda Owens, interviewed on BBC Radio Four, described gold medal-winning success as being 85–90 per cent psychological.[2]

And, as with sport, the main area of opportunity around developing your own potential for success is to do with the mind.

This mental factor is best summarised by the word 'resilience'. It captures attitude and mindset but also includes the extent to which we can bounce back from setbacks and persist with grit towards our goals. Resilience may sound a bit sporty and macho. It isn't. It's for everyone, regardless of gender or state of physical fitness. Further good news is that resilience is not fixed, not something with which you are either born or not. It can be built and the purpose of this book is to show you how.

Using the tools offered in this book will help you, just like an elite athlete, to build your own resilience development programme and enable you to get ready and persist towards achieving your goals, whatever life throws at you.

For the real lessons of elite performance in sports, we will look not just to the athletes themselves but also to the psychologists who have spent decades researching it.

Why? Because what they have discovered is that success is determined less by talent or innate ability and much more by effort. You will see in Chapter 3 that the relationship can be summarised as 2:1 – effort counts twice as much as innate ability. And yet the narrative outside sport that surrounds elite athletes so frequently attributes their success to their talent rather than their disciplined and dedicated training, often over decades.

We do this because it is liberating for us mere mortals who lack the appetite for such sustained hard work. In the same way, successful people in all walks of life appear born to the role, but their success, like that of athletes, is built on hard-won skills and a resilient mindset.

How can we be sure that resilience is so central to performance? Because it has been shown through scientific research to predict success in a range of pursuits. The point about science is an important one. Amid the abundance of books and YouTube videos out there on how to succeed, much of it has no basis in science. Indeed, some contradict what scientific research tells us. And by scientific research, I mean that it has passed the gold standard: publication in a peer-reviewed scientific journal, something that is only achieved with research that has been taken apart critically by fellow scientists, a long and painstaking process.

So the tools and techniques that we will go through in this book have a basis in science, something we will illustrate in each chapter under the heading 'Head science'.

How this book will help you build your own plan for success

This book maps out how to apply the new science of success in a practical and simple way. It will help you build a plan.

Part 1: Beliefs

We begin with the first dimension of building a resilient mindset for success: beliefs, negative or self-limiting ones in particular. Too often people fail in developing the performance needed to fulfil their goals, not because they lack talent or intellect but because they encounter setbacks and lose heart because of their beliefs.

Covering only enough of the theory as necessary, we will build a step-by-step programme for developing your own bounce-back-ability. We unpick some of the concepts often regarded as prerequisites for goal achievement and address some of the myths around how to build them. We then look at why negative thoughts and beliefs often inhibit us and offer a new mindset with which to approach our goals.

Part 2: Behaviours

The second dimension is about persistence and cultivating the ability to push on towards our long-term goals, resisting the temptation to procrastinate. Being able to do this and build your skills over time rather than opt for the easy way out is what predicts elite performance in a range of pursuits from sport to chess and musicianship.

If your past attempts to pursue goals have ended in quitting, then you will find tools and techniques in this part of the book that will help.

Part 3: Best practice

We build upon the fact that success for most of us is about cognition. How can we take the approach of an elite athlete to the pursuit of our goals? We look at treating the brain just as if it were a muscle and how to get the best out of it for sustained focus. We look at the habits and lifestyle that support a mindset for success and how to cultivate them.

These three components – beliefs, behaviours and best practice – will combine to form a practical personal development plan that will help you accomplish a step-change in performance and ultimately achieve success.

What this book is not

I've already mentioned the importance of a scientific evidence basis for the tools that I am going to introduce in this book. So I can promise that this book will be free of pseudoscience. At no point will I be suggesting that you can achieve success through simply thinking positive thoughts – there is no 'law of attraction' through which particles in the universe will align around your positivity and cause good things to happen.

By the same token, I will not be exhorting you to influence others through neuro-linguistic programming, something for which there is no evidence base.

This book will also not suggest to you any techniques to artificially boost your resilience, motivation or self-belief. Motivational quotes and videos abound on social media and illuminating though many of these are, they are of little help in and of themselves.

Rather than looking to 'amp' any of the above attributes, let's think of them a little like happiness. If you directly seek to boost your happiness, the exercise will often be futile. But if you pursue those dimensions of life that science tells us drive up happiness, such as meaningful work, life purpose, exercise, family, friends and community, happiness is an output. By following a plan based on science-based tools, you will find that confidence, motivation and self-belief will be a natural outcome.

Finally, this is not a 'life-hacking manual' – a hack is a software metaphor that suggests we can achieve success through some sort of back door in a programme's code. The tools we offer are not short-term hacks but long-term positive steps, that involve effort and commitment, towards building a resilient mindset for success.

What to expect when you read this book

Each chapter starts by describing a dimension of building a resilient mindset for success. But what happens when we don't have this attribute and how can it hold us back?

Next comes 'Head science', not a lecture in neuroscience or psychology but a simple explanation of how the way we are wired often inhibits us achieving great performance. Understanding this is half the battle.

The third component is where the rubber hits the road. This part of each chapter from Chapter 2 onwards involves activities and exercises that help illustrate a specific area of performance. It also includes tools and techniques that can be used as part of your overall Head Start plan. The first part of your development journey is to put your hands on a small book that you can use as a journal and for you to document your plan.

Along the way, there are case studies of people that I have worked with that will bring the concepts to life. I offer one or two examples from my own experience also.

Finally, we summarise each chapter with a bullet-point list of practical actions for you to incorporate into your development plan.

So, whatever your goal, whatever it is that you'd like to get better at, this is the perfect place to start. I want you to start thinking about this right now so your first step is to get a journal or notebook.

Think about your overarching goal. What would have to happen in five years' time for you to look back and think of yourself as having succeeded? Write it down.

For further resources go to www.headstartbook.com

Part 1

Beliefs

Chapter 1

Ten myths about achieving your goals

Addressing those myths

I could never do that!

If that's a thought that's ever held you back from attempting to fulfil a cherished ambition, then you're not alone. As we shall see, self-doubt is a pretty universal – and at one level, necessary – facet of our human wiring. Nevertheless, it can get in the way of achieving our goals. So often, it's not that we try and fail, it's that we don't have the confidence or self-belief to try in the first place. The word psychologists use for this is 'self-efficacy', the extent to which we believe that we can do something.

There is no simple, agreed, scientifically established way of overcoming this. If there were, we'd already be using it. As a result, there is an abundance of motivational posters, speakers and courses out there, all aimed at helping you along the road to success. While science doesn't yet have all the answers, it is making very rapid progress. However, much of what is out there, having no basis in science, is unhelpful. So, before we get into the detail of your Head Start programme, let's reframe the whole concept of what it takes to build a mindset for success by addressing a few myths.

Myth number 1: Goal achievement is determined by positive thinking

Books such as *The Power of Positive Thinking* and more recently *The Secret* would have us believe that the sheer act of thinking positively about a successful outcome and visualising this is enough to get us there. Psychological research has established that positive thinking and visualisation do not lead to any increased action towards our goals. While how we think about our goals and our challenges is important, there is much more to it than simply thinking positively – that is empty positive thinking.

Myth number 2: To achieve your goals, you're going to have to boost your confidence, motivation, passion or creativity

Right at the beginning of the book, I listed some negative beliefs that commonly hold us back. When we think about achieving our goals, whatever form they take, we focus on that elusive quality that we feel we're lacking. When we see successful people, they seem to exude confidence, energy and motivation. Our natural reaction might be to wish that we had such qualities and that, without them, we are unable to reach our goals. This is back to front thinking – it is so often the case that these qualities are outputs of a process that may have taken many years. By building their abilities, successful people often find that their confidence, motivation and passion all grow markedly.

For many people, the missing ingredient is confidence. They think of themselves as lacking in the quality that enables them to believe in themselves and go for it. Many people that I work with particularly feel this about themselves in the context of public speaking and presenting. Many in professional services that need to sell what they do identify confidence as a barrier to their sales efforts.

For others it's motivation: 'I'm lazy' or 'I start with good intentions and then I just end up watching *Game of Thrones*.'

For those with ambitions in creative fields, the desire is to somehow boost creativity so that they will be visited by a muse and be overwhelmed with inspiration.

There are many books, motivational YouTube videos and quotes on this subject, few of them with any scientific basis. As we shall see in the course of this book, it's best not to try and boost any of these qualities but to think of them as outputs or by-products of the programme we are going to put together.

Myth number 3: High achievers are confident

This may come as a surprise, but even some of the most successful people in the world experience lack of confidence some or all of the time. Let's look at a pursuit in which one might assume that confidence would be a very important attribute for a participant to have: sport. If you were to think of the highest achieving British sporting figures, which names might come up? How about the athletes that have accumulated the greatest number of Olympic golds?

Sir Chris Hoy has achieved six gold medals over successive Olympic Games and yet he sees the idea of the supremely confident athlete as a myth. Why? Because confidence is contextual. Sport brings with it so many variables that it would be impossible to be consistently confident all the time.

Chris Hoy experienced quite a dramatic loss of confidence at one point in his career, ultimately surmounting the problem using some of the tools in the next chapter.

Why do we assume that high-achieving people in sport and other pursuits are confident?

Well, some are. Some people do seem to have an innate level of self-belief that is impermeable, irrespective of what happens to them. This is not always healthy as it can make reflection difficult, and they sometimes fail to take responsibility for their own actions and do not always deal well with setbacks.

For others, there are two reasons why we make this assumption. The first is that many successful people have learned to project confidence consistently even when they may not feel it inside. We will come to this shortly. In sport, for example, it is not desirable to signal to your competitor that you are experiencing a crisis of self-doubt.

The second reason is that we have a psychological incentive to believe that all successful people are confident. Because if that's the case, then it must follow that because I lack confidence, success is out of my reach. Therefore, it would be futile to attempt it.

Both of these reasons are self-limiting beliefs. These are often deeply held because to challenge them is to take ourselves outside of our comfort zone.

Myth number 4: High achievers are consistently confident

Confidence is contextual. It will come and go according to circumstances that are frequently outside your control. As Chris Hoy says, when there is so much uncertainty and there are so many variables, you cannot be consistently confident.

Commenting on the 2017 Wimbledon tournament, Martina Navratilova – herself the winner of 18 Grand Slam titles – pointed out that even the top tennis players will experience ups and down in their confidence. She added that these ups and downs will happen even in the course of a single match.

Top athletes accept that confidence can fluctuate enormously and many have acquired the strategies needed to manage this. This book will introduce you to those strategies.

The fact is that confidence is actually something of a distraction. This book is not about directly boosting confidence. What it is about is helping you develop a resilient mindset from which success – and confidence – will be outputs. Developing your resilience for success will require you to place yourself outside your comfort zone, make yourself vulnerable and even set yourself up for the occasional setback. So there will be points in time when you will not be feeling confident. Building your resilience by its very nature involves putting yourself in situations in which your confidence will be low. What you will be doing is building your resilience. And that in turn will help you persist and succeed.

Myth number 5: Confidence is fixed – either you have it or you don't

Didn't I just say that some people have an innate level of confidence? Yes, that remains true. But that doesn't mean that that it cannot be grown. As we shall see throughout this book, there are very few skills and attributes that can't be built. Improved belief in your own ability to succeed in whatever field you choose to pursue will be an output of following the plan outlined in this book.

Myth number 6: Being positive or adopting a dominant posture will boost your confidence

Advice abounds about how to boost or amp your confidence – instantly. If it were really as simple as that, I would not be writing this book as those that feel inhibited by fear of failure would fix that simply by walking across hot coals, shouting 'I want to kill giants' at themselves in the mirror or standing feet apart and broad-shouldered in order to project a dominant posture.

We will come to the topic of positive thinking and how to use it to great effect in a science-based approach, which is so much more than simply being upbeat for its own sake. If you lack confidence, trying to boost it in this way is something psychologists call empty positive thinking.

As for dominant posturing, there is some scientific evidence that this does provide a small boost to confidence, something made popular in Amy Cuddy's TED talk about her own research[3] which is sound and has a good evidence base.

The scientifically established principle behind this effect is that the brain's communication with the rest of our body is a two-way channel. Not only will happiness cause us to smile, forming a smile will cause a small neurological effect that will increase our feeling of wellbeing. In her talk, Cuddy refers to the evidence that putting a pencil between our teeth causes a small spurt of feel-good neurochemicals in the brain – because the action of gripping the pencil causes the corners of the mouth to turn upwards as if we were smiling. This seems odd but it's true.

But the point here is that the effect is small and this is why trying to boost confidence artificially is a poor strategy. After all, if you were to get an appointment with your doctor for clinical depression, it would be less than helpful to be offered a pencil and told to grip it between your teeth. In the same way, empty positive thinking is to be avoided.

Myth number 7: If you don't have confidence, fake it until you make it

Some very distinguished people for whom I have a great deal of admiration have offered 'Fake it until you make it' as advice. Examples include Sheryl Sandberg and Amy Cuddy. This is a memorable exhortation with a neat rhyme but if you fear failure, the notion of faking it risks making you very uncomfortable to the point of experiencing anxiety.

In her book *Lean In*, Sheryl Sandberg (with co-writer Neil Scovell) talks of experiencing 'impostor syndrome' in her early career. You may recognise this feeling yourself if you have ever heard a voice in yourself telling you that you're about to get found out and finally be exposed as a fraud. If you recognise this, it is quite common and thought to be particularly so among women and ethnic minorities. But if you are experiencing thoughts about your status as a fraud, then it hardly helps to think of yourself as faking it.

There is a far better and science-based approach to building your belief in your ability succeed which we will come to in Chapter 3.

Confidence can be built. Following the personal development plan, that we are about to put together in this book, will help build it. But think of it less as an input – something that we need to acquire if we are to succeed – and more as an output, something that's a by-product of the behaviours that combine to make you successful. Confidence, like happiness or creativity, is part of the human experience that we experience when we are not looking directly for it. Try to boost it directly and we fail, but if we create the right conditions we can suddenly find that we have it after all.

Myth number 8: If you want to succeed, you've got to REALLY want it

My favourite YouTube motivational speaker is Eric Thomas, also known as the Hip Hop Preacher. He tells the parable of the ambitious young man who wanted to make money (and many of these videos are about the pursuit of money) and sought out a guru who had the secret of success. The guru asked the young man to meet him on the beach early the following morning. Puzzled, the young man turned up in his suit only to be led into the surf by the guru until they were waist-deep in sea water. The guru then grabbed the young man by the neck and pushed his head under water, holding it there until he was at the point of drowning.

When the young man was finally released, the guru asked him what he'd most wanted to do while being held underwater. When the young man replied that what he most wanted to do was breathe, the guru told him that when he wanted success as badly as he wanted to breathe, then that's when he was going to make it.

This parable does the rounds on social media in various forms and, while the story is memorable, this approach will not help with motivation. As with other mammals, our need to breathe is involuntary, controlled by our limbic system. In fact, it's almost impossible not to take a breath when we need one, whatever our level of motivation.

Hitting our goals will indeed require a level of self-motivation but the psychological process of building this is the opposite of what we do when we take a breath. Rather than being involuntary and unconscious, driving towards our goals is conscious and deliberate. Instead of trying to boost it through empty positive thinking, we are going to use evidence-based tools in order to build it.

Myth number 9: You need to find your one passion

What I've just said about motivation holds for passion. I often hear people express regret that they haven't yet found their passion in life. Many motivational talks I've attended in my business career have been given by people with an astonishing level of passion and single-minded focus.

A memorable talk by yachtswoman Dame Ellen MacArthur made a lasting impression on me as she described her early years trying to fund her first boat by saving her school dinner money. The anecdote that really stuck in my mind was her description of a solo round-the-world yacht race in which contestants ran into a life-threatening storm. One of her fellow contestants was so heavily battered by it that he bit off part of his tongue – and then, being alone, had to sew it back on.

Listening to this only made me reflect that I and the overwhelming majority of my colleagues would simply never have the same level of obsession for a pursuit where we might find ourselves sewing our own tongue back on.

Many high-achieving sportspeople in particular have this extremely high level of motivation from a very young age. It certainly helps but it's not a prerequisite for achieving our goals.

Sure, passion has a role to play but it's generally overstated. It's not something we necessarily need to have in vast quantities from the start but something that builds over time. In some respects, passion can even count against you. For entrepreneurs, it can limit cognitive flexibility and cloud commercial judgement.

Dilbert cartoonist Scott Adams had an early career in finance approving commercial loans for start-ups. He received some coaching from his boss to avoid lending to applicants that exhibited a passion in favour of 'grinders' with a more mundane sense of business reality and a solid business plan. This fits my own experience and the many successful entrepreneurs I have known – none has exhibited an elevated sense of passion about their business and all possess a commercial edge and often have a level of emotional detachment.

People I have worked with who have high levels of passion are often highly emotionally attached with the result that they lack cognitive flexibility and fail to recognise when something is not working. They will often persist – with a lot of passion – even when it is clear that things are not working out.

It's more important as you start to build your programme for goal achievement to simply be curious and to be open to new possibilities. Allow the passion to come to you.

Myth number 10: To get inspiration, you need to boost your creativity

If your goals are to do with the arts or other creative fields, you may feel that a barrier to achieving them is a lack of inspiration or creative insight. There are indeed ways of enhancing your creativity but lessons from some of the most famous artists tell us that such eureka moments are a by-product of something else: habitual, disciplined work. Great insights may arrive when they stop work, in moments of rest, but the work has to happen. As Pablo Picasso said: 'Inspiration exists, but it has to find you working.'

The important step here is to build the process that allows creativity to flourish.

The theme that emerges here when we look at a range of attributes that we might think of as prerequisites for success – be it confidence, motivation, passion or creativity – is that we need to think of them not as pre-existing qualities or aspects of personalities shared by successful people. If we do, and if we think of ourselves as lacking them, then we can inhibit our own capacity to succeed. As we shall see, rather than being qualities that successful people have, they are all outputs of building a mindset for success.

This chapter has addressed a number of myths that would be highly self-limiting if they were engrained as beliefs. We will now turn to the general area of negative self-talk, why it exists and what we can do about it.

Part 1: Examining your beliefs

Action	When
• If you haven't done so already, buy yourself a journal in which to make notes as you work through this book (or you may prefer to use your phone).	Now
• Read over the myths in this chapter. Make a note of your reaction to them. Write down any thoughts that come to mind. There is no need to judge your thoughts – just make a note of them.	Now

Chapter 2

Managing your negative emotional chatter

In Chapter 1 we mentioned the negative voice that says you can't do something or you're going to get found out. If you recognise this capacity for negative emotional chatter, often the source of our negative beliefs, then you're in good company as others experience it too. In fact, the entire human race does. You may find it reassuring to know that our brain is wired to do this.

Head science 2.1: Human brain version 1.0

The brain is an amazingly complex organ and one that still holds many mysteries that have yet to be yielded to scientists. However, recent advances in scanning technology and the combined efforts of neuroscientists and psychologists around the world are such that we have learned more about the brain in the last couple of decades than in the whole of human history.

The first important thing to understand about the brain is that it wasn't designed and manufactured in one go like the latest smartphone or electric car. Like its human owners, it has evolved over millions and millions of years with natural selection driving a myriad of small and subtle changes. This means that the brain is jerry-built. It's a little like a small bungalow to which successive rogue builders have added extensions over the years.

Fortunately, you do not need a degree in neuroscience to understand the way in which the brain works. Nor do you need to understand what every part of it does. We are going to focus on two distinct areas of the brain and their role in our success.

The limbic system

The first is the limbic system. It's the region of the brain that is the most primitive and includes components such as the amygdala which governs our fight-or-flight response in moments of physical danger. It's the part of the brain that evolved first, hence its position at the base of the skull. What is really important here is that it evolved when life for early humans and their ancestors was far less stable than it is now. Life was full of danger from natural threats, predators and other early humans. So the most important role of the brain was to keep us out of danger so that we could survive – at least long enough to reproduce and get our genes into the next generation.

Think of the limbic system as the emotional part of the brain. It still plays an important role in our survival. If you were to step out between parked cars and into the path of an oncoming bus, it's the limbic system that would cause you to step back on the kerb instinctively and instantly. If you do have the misfortune to have your head held underwater by a guru, it is your limbic system that makes you want to breathe.

But these moments of physical danger are rare in the twenty-first century so the emotional brain has to busy itself worrying about other potential sources of danger. Instead of sabre-toothed tigers and hostile tribal enemies, we have unseen fears – we may lose our job, there may be a downturn in the economy, our health may fail. This is before we take on all the global fears we can worry about courtesy of the 24/7 rolling news available on any number of channels. This includes but is not limited to world war, global terrorism, climate change and Brexit.

In this way, the emotional brain sees risk everywhere and wants us to avoid it. So those negative thoughts – the ones that tell you that you can't do something, that you don't have the talent, that it would be too risky and foolhardy to attempt it – are simply the emotional part of our brain doing its job and protecting us from danger.

The prefrontal cortex

The second part of the brain we need to know about arrived later and indeed has doubled in size over the last 500,000 years. That may seem like a very long time but in the world of evolution, it's just a blink of an eye. It's called the prefrontal cortex and is located on the edge of the brain behind our forehead. Cortex is Latin for 'edge' and as the outer part of the brain has grown, it has formed folds as a way of squeezing itself into the limited space of the skull. This explains the brain's crinkly surface.

The prefrontal cortex is the deep-thinking, analytical part of the brain. Unlike the limbic system, it is not driven by emotion. Instead it is rational, sensible and clear-sighted. It is responsible for planning and self-discipline.

It is also responsible for self-control and emotional management. This last part sometimes sets it at odds with the limbic system.

Inner conflict

In fact, much of our inner turmoil can be explained by these two parts of our brain being in conflict, a little like two ill-suited flatmates that don't get on terribly well. Let's take that metaphor a little further – I think of these flatmates as male although the ones in your own head may well be female.

The guy who moved in first is big, aggressive, scruffy, loud and bullying; he has a bedroom but seems to spend all his time in the main room, sleeping on the sofa and generally having the run of the place. Let's call him 'Sofa-Man'. This is the emotional part of our brain or the limbic system. Long, long after this resident got settled in and got used to having the place to himself, a flatmate moved in to the spare bedroom as a lodger. He's a more thoughtful, considerate but rather small and weedy chap. This is the prefrontal cortex and we'll refer to him as 'The Lodger'.

By the front door of the flat is a whiteboard on which both flatmates get to write things. What is written there are not the domestic duties of flat-sharing such as the washing-up rota or a reminder not to raid the fridge and eat one another's food. The whiteboard is where our beliefs are written. And our success is going to be very much determined by who has control of the whiteboard.

This relationship between the brain's two co-habitants defines the two fundamental reasons why people so often do not ultimately succeed in achieving their goals.

THE LIMBIC SYSTEM IS STRONGER

When it comes to fulfilling our ambitions and reaching our goals, it is The Lodger, the thoughtful, deep-thinking guy in the second bedroom that makes this happen. The trouble for The Lodger is that Sofa-Man wants us to avoid risk and save our energy for when danger arrives. So he opts for an easy life, spurning effort and preferring to lounge on the sofa and binge-watch box sets while drinking beer and eating pizza.

As we shall see, success is determined by the ability to persist towards our goals and bounce back from setbacks rather than opt for the risk-free easy option. The first of the two problems that we confront is that Sofa-Man is far stronger than The Lodger. In terms of brain science, the limbic system has lots of powerful chemicals called neurotransmitters that it can use in its conflict with the prefrontal cortex. So, when The Lodger tries to assert some discipline and move you away from short-term attractions, he ends up being bullied into submission by his flatmate. When this happens, The Lodger sits meekly in his room with the door shut listening to Sofa-Man's loud music booming through the wall.

ALL NEWS GOES THROUGH THE LIMBIC SYSTEM

When The Lodger is closeted in the room with the door shut, there is no contact with the outside world, not even access to wifi. It's Sofa-Man that answers the front door so he first receives any news or gets to hear about important events. While The Lodger will take a reasoned and balanced approach to important events, Sofa-Man is, as we said earlier, emotional and negative. So the interpretation – particularly of any bad news – is likely to be catastrophic.

Remember the whiteboard by the front door? If The Lodger is locked in his bedroom, then Sofa-Man gets first dibs at writing up his interpretation of whatever news has just been received. This interpretation will inevitably be negative and make The Lodger even more timid.

A flourishing prefrontal cortex

This metaphor of the brain as having two conflicting flatmates is one to which we will return frequently as success is so much driven by our ability to build and maintain a flourishing prefrontal cortex. This means that The Lodger needs to be strong enough to keep Sofa-Man under control and sitting quietly where he belongs, on the sofa or, better still, in his own room. For The Lodger, it also means having control of the whiteboard so that it doesn't get covered in the untidy negative beliefs and fears that Sofa-Man likes to write.

Increasing our self-awareness

The first stage in our personal development plan is not to change the way in which our brain works. That comes later. Let us start with just being self-aware.

We've described the way the emotional part of the brain works and used the metaphor of the flat-share to bring it to life. We've described Sofa-Man as being very negative and catastrophic and you may experience this as a constant stream of impulsive mental chatter, thoughts that simply pop up as you go through your day in response to whatever you encounter.

Our emotional brain is very judgemental. Sometimes this is turned on those we see around us. So as we travel to work or push a trolley around the supermarket, we may experience negative thoughts about others popping into our head – the driver in front of us who hasn't realised the lights have changed because they're looking at their phone, or the person in front of us in the supermarket queue who can't find their loyalty card.

But it's also often turned inwards, on ourselves. When something at work doesn't go right or if we experience a loss at the competitive sport we play, we can experience a stream of negative mental chatter.

EXERCISE 2.1: YOUR EMOTIONAL BRAIN

The first task is to capture these mutterings from our emotional brain. I asked you in the introduction to think about your overarching goal and what would have to happen in five years' time for you to look back and feel that you have succeeded. Look at what you wrote down. Now tune into what the emotional part of your brain, your own Sofa-Man/Woman, is saying. Write down those thoughts.

For the next few days carry your journal with you and write down the language your emotional brain uses. There's no need to share this so be as raw as you like, including swear words. The more literally you can capture these emotional mutterings, the greater will be your level of self-awareness.

As you carry on reading and carrying out the Head Start plan, keep up this journal for a week and then review. What do you notice about the thoughts you've captured? Make a note of any themes or patterns.

Putting distance between ourselves and our emotional brain

If we lack self-awareness, we risk allowing all the mutterings from our emotional brain to become engrained without being filtered or challenged. This is as if Sofa-Man has taken complete control of the whiteboard by the front door and writes down whatever comes into his head. As you will have found out, these thoughts and beliefs are often negative, judgemental and catastrophising.

'Catastrophising' is the word psychologists use to describe the process of thinking that everything is going to hell in a handcart or, in other words, that everything is going (or is about to go) wrong. For anyone aiming to make progress towards a long-term challenging goal, often involving personal risk of some sort, catastrophising is not a helpful activity, particularly if it is unwarranted.

The next exercise is the first step towards rectifying this. And it's among the most simple and yet powerful tools that this book offers. I want to you to sustain the level of self-awareness that you have now achieved after practising Exercise 2.1. After doing it for a week, you should have a heightened sense of awareness of when it is your emotional brain that is behind any given thought or emotion.

EXERCISE 2.2: CONTROLLING NEGATIVE THOUGHTS

What I want you to do next is play back each negative thought as soon as you become aware of it. But as you play the words back to yourself in your head, I want you to insert the following words at the beginning: 'My emotional brain is saying that...'

These simple preceding words have an important impact. They put distance between you and the mutterings of your emotional brain. So for The

Lodger, rather than be cowed by his flatmate and give up control of the whiteboard by the front door, this means acknowledging the emotional thoughts and beliefs that he will hear from time to time. It's just Sofa-Man muttering, doing what he does.

We will never stop the emotional part of our brain from causing some of these thoughts to pop into our heads. It is a fundamental part of our neurological wiring and we simply have to accept that this is the way we have evolved for reasons of survival. What we can do, however, is choose how we respond to these thoughts. And in the battle between our limbic system and our prefrontal cortex – and I'm afraid that it is a battle – there is much we can do to stack the odds in favour of the latter.

Stop drinking from the bad news firehose

Remember that we said that Sofa-Man gets to answer the front door? This is important because this negative, catastrophising individual will gleefully seize on any evidence that can be spun to support the belief that the world is going to hell in a handcart. Some of this negativity is about the external environment but it can become infectious and self-directed. Once the emotional part of the brain becomes fraught with negativity, it can bleed into how we feel about ourselves and cause us to lose confidence. After all, our emotional brain wants to prevent us from taking risks and preserve energy.

The brain's wiring made perfect sense in the environment in which our ancestors evolved some 100,000 years ago. In the twenty-first century, however, the abundance of channels on which we can receive the latest disastrous news is such that Sofa-Man is constantly rushing from the sofa to the front door and then wailing about it to The Lodger.

I remember driving to a client workshop in the north-east of England in 2011 as the European currency crisis was at its height with riots taking place in Greece and debt crises in other countries such as Spain and Italy. I decided to tune in to news coverage of these significant geopolitical events and after three hours of listening to experts very convincingly paint a picture in which the world economy was about to disintegrate, I came very close to pulling into a service station and filling the car to the brim with bottled water and canned food.

Several years later, while the financial problems in Greece are not necessarily behind us, it has been displaced in the news by other scare stories and the world has not ended. But at the time, my own Sofa-Man was battening down the hatches and propelling me into a bunker.

The two problems with the news is first, that it is everywhere and second, that it is almost universally bad. As psychologist Steven Pinker says: 'Journalists report plane crashes, not planes that take off. As long as bad things haven't vanished from the earth altogether, there will always be enough of them to fill the news. And people will believe, as they have for centuries, that the world is falling apart.'[4]

The ubiquity of bad news is partly a result of the way in which media and technology have developed causing us to be in constant communication with one another and with news outlets. As a default on my smartphone, if I swipe right with my thumb the very first thing presented to me is a series of news headlines. As I write, the first is about the storm that has battered Britain overnight. If I engage with others on social media I will see news items retweeted. Turning on the TV or radio will also expose me to news flashes and periodic news updates.

People often observe that we rarely hear good news. There are two reasons for this. First, it would be impractical for the news to report all the flights that landed safely each day or the pop concerts that ended without a terrorist attack. Second, for reasons that we've already discussed, consumers want bad news. In our ancestral environment, being the first to find out about threats to our safety, whether these were from marauding tribal enemies or food sources that would make us ill, meant that we were more likely to survive, reproduce and get our genes into the next generation.

Publishers of newspapers and broadcasters know this. For this reason, it will feel alien at first to cut yourself off but I recommend a 'news fast'.

EXERCISE 2.3: NEWS FAST

This means not exposing yourself to the negative litany of global disasters. Instead of listening to talk radio in the car, put on some enjoyable music. Rather than pick up a newspaper before jumping on the train, read a book. Also limit your time on social media to a small number of time slots.

Inevitably, you will experience an uneasy feeling that you are missing out. And yes, it is just possible that you will be the last to hear when the next global music superstar shuffles off this mortal coil. But does this matter if managing your emotional reactivity helps you succeed in reaching your goals? In any case, that missing-out feeling will soon pass and you will find that the emotional part of your brain a little less animated. Sofa-Man is much more likely to remain sitting on the sofa placidly if the supply of bad news to the front door is cut off.

Once you have experienced the news fast for a while, then you can expose yourself to news in a measured and limited way. I have a newspaper delivered at weekends and love to scour the latest articles over a leisurely breakfast. But that's it. No radio or TV news, no looking at anyone's Twitter feed. I use Google alerts to update me about anything that might be of professional importance but that is it.

In Chapter 4 we will come to the nature of optimism and its importance in building a successful and positive mindset. Exposing yourself to a constant stream of bad news is not only bad for your equanimity, it's also misleading.

It turns out that in spite of all the worst fears of the doomsayers, the world is, by just about any measure you care to use, getting better. Not only are we all living longer and with a better quality of life, the world is getting less violent. This may seem an unlikely assertion but there is a solid evidence base behind it.

Steven Pinker's book *The Better Angels of our Nature* documents this trend compellingly. If you haven't got the appetite to read a lengthy book, read the transcription of the Munk Debate on the motion: *Do Humankind's Best Days Lie Ahead?* Pinker delivers a brief but compelling opening statement in support of the motion in which he refers to all the data demonstrating solid, long-term improvements in life expectancy, disease eradication, prosperity, peace, safety, freedom, human rights, gender equality and intelligence.

American science-fiction writer William Gibson once said: 'The future is already here – It's just not very evenly distributed.' Long-term positive trends are of little comfort to anyone caught up in the midst of a civil war, but the fact remains that there is plenty to be optimistic about. In place of drinking from the fire hose of 24/7 news, invest some time reading the works of social scientists and others that have built the case for optimism.

Part 2: Managing your negative emotional chatter

Action	When
• Keep a diary for a week to capture your emotional chatter. Write down your thoughts in the raw language in which they pop into your head. Note at what or whom these thoughts are directed.	For the next week
• Put some distance between you and your emotional brain. As a negative thought pops into your head, play it back to yourself but first insert the words: 'The emotional part of my brain is saying that...'	From week 2 onwards
• Start a news fast. Avoid watching or listening to broadcast news and reduce your exposure to other sources such as social media.	From now on
• Read books such as *Do Humankind's Best Days Lie Ahead?* and *The Better Angels of Our Nature* by Stephen Pinker or *Non-Zero* by Robert Wright to promote your optimism about the world.	In the future

Chapter **3**

Reframing your beliefs by building a growth mindset

Challenging negative beliefs

Remember the whiteboard by the front door of our flat? This is where negative, catastrophising Sofa-Man gets to write up all manner of negative beliefs when he's not sitting quietly on the sofa.

Many of these negative beliefs revolve around our own ability to achieve our goals. We mentioned a common one right at the beginning of the book: 'I could never do that.'

Other common negative beliefs include:

- I'm not good enough.

- I simply don't have the talent.

- I'm not a natural x (where x is a job, function, personality trait, sports player or artist).

- If it were going to happen, it would have happened by now.

The trouble with negative beliefs is that they can become self-fulfilling. And our emotional brain loves them. Why? Because they inhibit us from taking risks, making ourselves vulnerable and exposing us to failure. Remember that for evolutionary reasons, our emotional brain is wired to drive us away from risk because our ancestral environment was so dangerous and full of mortal danger. So we need to challenge these negative beliefs and alter our mindset when it comes to our own abilities.

Reframe the concept of talent

The first step is to reframe the concept of talent and the extent to which our success is or is not determined by whether or not we were born with innate ability. This is an area where social scientists have worked for decades and their conclusions have important lessons for us.

My favourite example of a sporting icon that appears to have been endowed with more than her fair share of talent is Japanese figure skater, Shizuka Arakawa. While not necessarily a household name in the West, she won the World Championships in 2004 and Olympic gold in 2006. You can catch a glimpse of her in rehearsal at those Olympic Games on YouTube here (Google 'Shizuka Arakawa triple triple' to find the clip). You do not have to be an expert in figure skating to appreciate the grace of her moves as she executes a triple salchow, a triple toe and a triple loop in succession. Even the experienced commentators are spellbound. If you listen carefully, you will hear one of them say: 'She was born to skate!'

But what makes Arakawa so interesting is not so much her achievement but the journey she took to get there. She is singled out by Geoff Colvin in his book *Talent is Overrated* because her effortless grace belies the effort that went into acquiring it. Colvin conducted an analytical exercise on Arakawa's practice regime over her career and came up with an estimate of the number of times she fell over on the ice in the course of her twenty-year progression to Olympic gold. Any ideas? Have a guess. Write down the first number that comes to you.

The answer: Geoff Colvin's estimate for the number of tumbles is 20,000. Even if he has over-estimated by a factor of two, then that's still quite a lot of falls. So when we talk about falling on your backside, few people will have done more of it than Shizuka Arakawa.

Imagine that you were a casual passer-by at an ice rink where Arakawa was practising at any point in her career. Without knowing anything about her or her successful future, imagine her seeing her fall over as she tried one of her signature triple manoeuvres. Maybe more than once. What might your reaction have been? I might have said to myself that she wasn't very good or obviously wasn't cut out for figure skating.

The point Colvin made using Arakawa's example is that talent is something of a myth. We use it to explain the success of others and downplay the importance of sustained hard work and training. But that is often an excuse and a way for us to avoid putting in similar levels of effort.

Friedrich Nietzsche put this elegantly as long ago as the nineteenth century.

> **'For if we think of genius as something magical, we are not obliged to compare ourselves and find ourselves lacking... To call someone "divine" means: "here there is no need to compete."'**

Writers such as Geoff Colvin and Matthew Syed have caused us to reassess the very concept of talent and have pointed to the evidence of what has instead been shown by science to predict success, not just in sport but in other pursuits.

But before we let go of the concept of talent, is there no such thing as innate ability? There is, but when we think of someone as talented what is innate is the ease with which they can acquire new skills. We have probably all experienced this from childhood onwards. When taking up a new sport, some people seem to pick up the skills right away while for others it feels unnatural.

I had my own experience of this when I took up tennis with my wife when we were both in our mid-forties, never having played before. I should add that this book will feature a few examples from tennis – not just because it happens to be the one sport that I play actively but because it lends itself particularly well, for reasons that we will discover, to the whole area of resilience and goal achievement.

We had joint beginner lessons in which our coach showed us how to do a double-handed backhand, something to me that felt very unnatural and awkward. When he started feeding us balls, my attempts were pretty disastrous. I felt as if I were wielding a large stick. My wife, on the other hand, from the first ball, whacked her backhands to the opposite corner of the court in classic low-to-high, finishing-over-the-shoulder style. She looked like a professional. As for me, I did finally nail it. After eight years of coaching every weekend.

On the other hand, we can possibly all think of promising athletes that are able to acquire the skills quickly but are not interested in putting in the effort to train. Nick Kyrgios is a prominent example in tennis. 'I'm not dedicated to the game at all,' he said in 2017. In spite of their early promise, these talented athletes that acquire skills easily but do not work on them in a disciplined way often fail to flourish.

Leading positive psychology exponents such as Martin Seligman have a simple way of explaining the role of both talent and hard work in high achievement. They make a clear distinction between the two but emphasise that effort counts twice.

What do they mean by this? The first way that effort counts is that you have to employ it with your innate ability in order to acquire the skills of your sport or pursuit. So, however easy it is for you to acquire the skills, effort is needed on top of the skills in order to deliver a great performance.

Laid out as a formula it looks like this:

Talent + Effort = Skills

Skills + Effort = Achievement

So effort counts twice!

Case study

Lee was one of my workshop attendees in London where he worked in corporate support for a global financial services organisation. While the workshop was about cognitive performance in the workplace, he found it hard to move on from this reframed idea of talent because of his personal experience.

'I took up the guitar a while ago,' he explained. 'And right from the outset, I found it really hard stretching the fingers of my left hand on the fretboard to make chords. It felt unnatural and difficult. It struck me that I simply didn't have the natural ability to form these chords. So I gave up.'

To help Lee reframe his mindset, we discussed how there was a possibility that a famous virtuoso guitar player – say Andrés Segovia – found the whole process of forming chords much easier at the outset. Indeed, this seems likely as Segovia was regarded as having an aptitude for music at an early age and first performed publicly at 16. But many other accomplished guitarists will have found the same experience as Lee. Rather than give up, they persisted in building their abilities.

Lee resolved to revisit his guitar playing with a new mindset. I look forward to receiving my invitation to his first recital.

Head science 3.1: Fixed versus growth mindset

Something psychologist Carol Dweck has discovered is that your ability to grow and build your skills at anything depends to a large extent upon your beliefs about the nature of talent and ability. If you believe that what you can do is determined by your genetic inheritance, then Dweck describes this as having a 'fixed' mindset.[5] Guess which part of the brain likes to act as a cheerleader for the fixed side of the argument. That's right, it's our emotional brain.

Because Sofa-Man wants us to avoid risk, he will, if unchallenged, write in big capitals on the whiteboard that you were not cut out to do whatever it is you aspire to do. And he will gleefully look for any failure or setback as evidence of this.

Carol Dweck showed this process in action with schoolchildren. In her research she took a sample of children about to make the transition to junior high school and measured their mindsets using a psychometric test. What were their beliefs about their own intelligence? Did they think of them as something that could be fixed or something that could be developed?

This gave her two groups with the same academic achievement, but one had a fixed mindset while the other a 'growth' one. Dweck picked this transition point because this is where school gets tougher – it's when teachers hold your hand to a lesser extent and when grades begin to suffer. But not all pupils' grades suffer equally. When she interviewed the fixed mindset pupils to understand why they believed their grades were suffering, they either blamed themselves ('I suck at math') or somebody else, such as their teacher, often with colourful language such as 'Because the teacher is on crack.'

This shows that even with young children, it is your beliefs about how fixed your abilities are that determine the extent to which you can change them. With a fixed mindset, challenges and obstacles are simply an affirmation that we don't have the talent and we are therefore more likely to quit in order to save face. Criticism is something we fear and avoid as it will reflect negatively on us.

By contrast, those with a growth mindset seek out challenges in order to stretch themselves as part of their learning experience; similarly, they thrive on feedback to help them along the path towards mastery. Obstacles and plateaux are not signals to quit but barriers to success that need to be overcome.

Head science 3.2: The truth about child prodigies

One scientist has invested his entire career in studying high achievement in a range of disciplines including sport, chess, musicianship and creative arts. His name is Anders Ericsson and his conclusions make interesting reading when it comes to our beliefs about talent[6].

We think of child geniuses and prodigies as someone like Mozart but the child prodigy is something of a myth. You might be troubled by the idea that Mozart's precocious ability does not make him a child prodigy and a poster-child for the concept of natural talent. After all, isn't it a matter of historical record that young Wolfgang was wowing audiences across Europe with his harpsichord playing at age 6 and composing symphonies by the age of 11?

What was sensational at the time was the idea of a child of six playing a musical instrument so well. This becomes less sensational when Ericsson points out that Wolfgang's father Leopold Mozart was himself a professional musician with very progressive beliefs about teaching music to children at a very early age. This is what he did with his own children.

Now, however, this is not regarded as unusual. The popular Suzuki method for teaching the playing of musical instruments to children of two or even younger means that there is an abundance of modern Wolfgangs as a search in YouTube will quickly demonstrate.

What about the child composer? Wolfgang's early concertos were, as Ericsson points out, in Leopold's handwriting. His other compositions, while once believed to be original, turned out to be re-workings of other contemporary pieces, often again with a lot of extra work from Leopold.

So while it may be deflating to prick the bubble surrounding historic geniuses such as Mozart, the truth about talent should come as great encouragement to your pursuit of excellence and high achievement, whatever your field.

The fact is, whatever the ease with which he acquired new musical skills, Mozart's extraordinary achievement at such a young age is explained to a large extent by the fact that he was immersed in practice while very young by his father.

We can see many twenty-first century successors to this principle, particularly in sport. Richard Williams writes in his remarkable autobiography *Life in Black and White* that he suggested his wife have two more daughters so that he could produce two tennis aces. He went on to write a 78-page plan on doing this before Venus and Serena were even born.

Ericsson has studied elite achievement in a wide range of fields from sport, virtuoso musicianship and chess. His conclusion is that at the very top level, the only distinction between the very best of the best and their less accomplished peers is this: the amount of time spent in deliberate practice.

Studying a cohort of aspiring concert violinists, Ericsson plotted the number of hours they had clocked up in practice as they got older. He found that by the age of 20, the best violinists had accumulated 10,000 hours of solitary practice. You may have come across this as 'The Ten Thousand Hour Rule', as popularised by Malcolm Gladwell who pointed out that the Beatles had put in roughly this amount of time playing in Hamburg and that Bill Gates spent a similar length of time honing his programming skills.

Ericsson stresses that there is no magic threshold at 10,000 hours. The violinists were by no means the finished article at 20 but his analysis produced a nice round number at that age. As they continued to develop, the number of hours continued to accumulate.

There is, it turns out, a linear relationship between achievement and the time spent in purposeful practice. This specific form of practice is something we will come to in Chapter 5 in more detail. Right now, we are focusing on reframing our beliefs about talent.

Head science 3.3: The surprisingly adaptable human

Our capacity as a species to grow and get better at whatever it is we decide to do is remarkable. Ericsson gives as an example the pursuit of the world record in press-ups. How many can you do in one go? I'm not a drill sergeant so I'm not asking you to drop to the floor and give me ten. But write down how many you think you could do in one go? 20? 50? Now write down what you think the world record might be.

The answer, set by Minoru Yoshida in 1980, is 10,507. This was the last time that the Guinness Book of Records accepted submissions for this pursuit. Why? Because the reason contestants were stopping was not fatigue but the need to go to the toilet. So the record was changed to allow breaks and now reflects the number of press-ups in a 24-hour period. At the time of writing, the record is held by Charles Servizio of the US and stands at 46,001.

This is heartening if your ambitions revolve around a physical activity. People often ask me in workshops how likely they would be to beat Usain Bolt over 100 metres if they were to take up sprinting in adulthood. While a victory over Bolt is unlikely, what I point out is likely is that, were you to join an athletics club and embrace a disciplined training regime, you could certainly steadily improve your performance. You would be a far better sprinter in six months' time than you are today.

If your goals are to do with a knowledge pursuit such as writing, speaking or building a business, then there is equally encouraging scientific evidence for the adaptability of the brain.

The hippocampus is a small part of the brain in two parts, one on each side, each part shaped a little bit like a seahorse. The word hippocampus is Latin for seahorse. The hippocampus plays an important part in spatial memory and navigation.

A study in 2000 by neuroscientist Eleanor Maguire and her colleagues conducted brain-imaging studies of a group of London black cab drivers and compared the size of the hippocampus to that of a sample of the general population.[7] It turned out that the posterior part of the hippocampus was far larger than that of the general sample. What's more, the longer the cab drivers had been in their job, the larger this part of the brain was.

Why this remarkable change to the brain? The answer is that in order to get their licence (or their 'badge') London cab drivers have to do something known as the Knowledge, a study of London's tens of thousands of streets and a large number of routes on which they are examined. This can take years. My father was a cabbie and it took him two and a half years going around the capital on a moped before he acquired his cherished green badge.

The fact is that while we might think of our brain as fixed, like the human body it is surprisingly adaptable. If we choose to throw ourselves at whatever is our equivalent of press-ups, then our brain will adapt accordingly.

For sports, frequent disciplined practice of techniques causes them to be honed to the point that they are almost instinctive. In the brain, synapses – connections between neurons – are established and strengthened. A sheath made of a substance called myelin wraps itself around the synapses and it is this that causes the skills to be hardwired. The expression 'What fires together, wires together' is a reference to this process in the brain.

Just like the body, the brain is remarkably adaptable. We tend to think of it as fixed and compartmentalised into a number of separate regions, all with their distinct functions. The truth is that the brain is much more flexible than we think. More is being understood all the time about something called neuroplasticity, the capacity of the brain to change shape, not just chemically but even structurally. Our brains change shape whenever we study or learn something new. I expect yours is changing right now as you read this.

Building your own growth mindset

When you approach your own goals, a growth mindset will help you quieten down the negative, hypercritical mutterings of Sofa-Man. If you have a fixed mindset and believe that your talent is innate, criticism is something to be feared because it threatens your belief in your ability. With a growth mindset, we thrive on criticism. We actively seek it out because it will help us build our skills. And we don't take it personally because the criticism is not directed at us as a person but on our efforts to get better.

EXERCISE 3.1: FIXED MINDSET MUTTERINGS

Just as in Chapter 2 when I asked you to keep a journal of your own Sofa-Man's negative mutterings, I'd like you to take this a step further. Now, listen out particularly carefully for fixed mindset mutterings. Make a note in your journal as and when you notice them. Be as literal as possible.

Your fixed mindset mutterings will often be directed inwardly in the shape of sentiments that we mentioned at the beginning of the chapter. But you might also find Sofa-Man undermining your own capacity to succeed by coming up with misleading explanations for the success of others. If you are aware of people that have made great strides in the area in which you would like to succeed yourself, Sofa-Man – motivated by jealousy and not wishing to confront the uncomfortable fact that you could achieve the same thing – will explain away the success of others. 'They're lucky because their parents gave them a head start' or 'They got started at a time when it was much easier to make a living doing that.'

Instead, use your growth mindset to find out what it is that high achievers did in order to build their skills. When you examine the careers of high achievers in almost any field you care to think of, it is rarely the case that they became successful overnight. Their eventual success came after sustained periods of effort and purposeful practice.

Psychologist Eduardo Briceno put this best in his 2012 TEDx talk on the growth mindset: 'Listen out for your fixed mindset voice. If you hear it say: "I can't do that," add the word, "yet"'[8].

Case study

Graham ran a small consulting firm and was struggling to grow revenues outside his traditional client base in the aviation sector. I helped him and his small team of consultants reframe their attitude to sales. Before this happened, they observed that one of their team, Geoff, seemed to find selling much easier than his peers. 'It's easy for Geoff,' the others were saying. 'He's got a much bigger network than we have.' They had all adopted this belief to the point that, for the rest of them, it was simply impossible for them to succeed in selling.

Part of the turnaround rested on getting the team to recognise this sentiment as fixed mindset talk that had taken hold among the whole ▶

team – except, of course, Geoff. Even Graham believed that selling was pretty much futile for the rest of them. It was true that Geoff did have a big network because of his experience and the length of his career.

We needed a change of mindset and I got the team to reorient their attitude. 'What's my plan,' they began to ask themselves, 'for building a network like Geoff's? How can I learn from what Geoff's achieved? What are the specific actions I'm going to take?'

Put yourself out there

While resilience is critical for helping us bounce back from adversity, we need another component in order to build a mindset for success – the willingness to take on challenge. This is where having a growth mindset is so important.

Whatever pursuit you would like to get better at and wherever you are in life, the science tells us that you can get better at it and achieve great things. Clearly, it helps to have got your purposeful practice in from a very young age. 'I wish my mum had forced me to play the piano when I was a child,' said Dudley Moore when in character as Dud in an early Dud and Pete sketch. Ironically, Moore did study the piano as a child and secured a place at Magdalen College, Oxford on an organ scholarship.

It turns out there are very few pursuits where starting at a young age is an actual requirement. When Anders Ericsson spoke in London in 2016 he mentioned ballet as one example and the subject of one of his studies. If dancers do not learn pointe at an early age, the growth plates in their feet become fused and it becomes much harder. He also mentioned the pitching motion of baseball players as needing to be mastered before the onset of puberty, otherwise it becomes physically impossible for the adult shoulder to support the full motion.

Sadly for my own sporting career, the same is true of the tennis serve. But apart from these examples, there are no inherent physical reasons why you cannot build your skills if you did not start in childhood. And even with this limitation, you can become a great late starter at ballet, baseball or tennis – or all three.

Part of building a growth mindset is about feeling comfortable with making yourself vulnerable. Sofa-Man will continue to scribble thoughts of the 'I-could-never-do-that!' type on your belief-system whiteboard but sometimes you can surprise yourself.

I like to take my own medicine and I recently decided to put this to the test and had a go at something I had previously said I would simply never attempt, something that filled me with terror: stand-up comedy. Laughing Horse has run comedy courses for almost 20 years and on a cold weekend in January, together with an old friend called Jack, I enrolled on a two-day crash course in stand-up with comedian Jay Sodagar. Late on a Sunday evening, my classmates and I each performed a five-minute set in a room above a pub in West London. Admittedly, the audience was almost entirely made up of the rest of the class and their immediate family (including a babe in arms) but we all did it. Sadly, my brief set was not recorded and is therefore lost to posterity but even I don't think it was all that bad. I even got some laughs.

Every time that we make ourselves vulnerable, take on a challenge or do something risky, there is a risk that it will backfire on us. The fact is, if our goals are truly stretching and ambitious, we are going to encounter setbacks along the way. This is why the next chapter is all about giving us the tools to bounce back.

But what about doing more than just bouncing back? Bouncing back suggests taking us to where we were before the setback happened. What about the Nietzschian ideal of 'what does not kill me makes me stronger'? In the book *Option B*,[9] Adam Grant and Sheryl Sandberg offer the idea of 'bouncing forward', learning from a setback and becoming stronger as a result. They quote research by psychologists Richard Tedeschi and Lawrence Calhoun into post-traumatic stress and found that even among parents grieving for children that had died, there was evidence of post-traumatic growth. Tedeschi and Calhoun offer a slightly milder mantra than Nietzsche's: 'I am more vulnerable than I thought, but much stronger than I ever imagined.'[10]

The fact is that taking a growth mindset to just about anything can have surprising results.

Part 3: Building a growth mindset

Action	When
• Ask yourself where you have a fixed mindset, particularly when it comes to the ambitions or dreams that drew you to this book. Make a note in your journal of the fixed mindset beliefs that you currently hold.	Now
• Add to your diary any fixed mindset thoughts that pop into your head. Remember to capture the language in its raw state.	From now on
• Start to build a growth mindset plan. Who has achieved great things in this area that I can learn from? How can I get feedback in order to grow my abilities? Where can I find challenges to help me learn and hone my skills?	Now
• Find something that feels well outside your comfort zone and give it a go, even if it makes you feel vulnerable to do so. Look for a weekend course for beginners that offers a safe environment. Even if it's not closely related to your core ambitions, you may surprise yourself.	In the future

Chapter 4

Dealing with setbacks

Failure and the need to cope with it

In whatever field we pursue success we are at some point going to confront failure. This can take many forms: being passed over for promotion at work, not being picked for a sports team, a start-up business that hits a cash crisis or a failed driving test.

This is where we most need resilience, the quality that allows us to bounce back and carry on towards our goals. Without resilience, our confidence can be shattered and this lack of confidence can cause us to avoid exposing ourselves to such situations again. As we shall see, this is a natural human response and part of our wiring. Reassuringly, there are tools that can help us bounce back.

Take the example of Andy Murray

Andy Murray's tennis career offers a great example of how even the most successful performers have had to overcome adversity. With the benefit of hindsight – and having witnessed Murray become world number one, win multiple Grand Slams, two Olympic gold medals and play a central part in Great Britain's 2015 Davis Cup victory – it is easy to forget the difficulty he faced as recently as 2012 when he had yet to win a Grand Slam.

'To be frank,' Murray writes in his autobiography, 'at that stage of my career, I was feeling like I was a loser: Nothing more, nothing less. You wouldn't believe the abuse I would get walking down the street: people would swear and shout at me. If I went on Twitter, there was a ridiculous amount of abuse. I felt like a failure.'[11]

What was it that had caused Murray to feel like a failure? He had reached four Grand Slam finals and lost each of them. It would have been easy for him at this point to lose heart. After all, he was losing to players of the quality of Roger Federer and Novak Djokovic, arguably two of the finest players of all time and both seemingly implacable in such finals. Should he at this point have settled for the consolation prize of fulfilling the traditional role of plucky British loser?

Pivotal in Murray's success in overcoming what seemed an impassable blockage was recruiting Ivan Lendl as his coach. He had also lost his first four Grand Slam finals so his impact was less to do with the skills, techniques or tactics of Murray's game and much more to do with his mindset. As Murray writes:

'He's made me learn more from losses than maybe I did in the past... And when I've lost matches, he's not necessarily negative. After the 2012 Wimbledon final he told me he was proud of the way I played because I went for it when I had chances. It was the first time I played like that in a Grand Slam final. He's altered my mentality going into those sort of matches.'

While Murray had tried to use psychologists to help with mindset earlier in his career, it was only when Lendl introduced him to Alexis Castorri, who he had used himself at the same point in his own career, that a breakthrough was achieved.

Castorri had built her reputation on helping athletes cope with the way in which they view negative events. As her brother Rob says: 'The therapy she deals in is based around the fact you cannot affect what happens to you but you have freedom in life to choose the attitude you take to the things that happen.'[12]

We know from history that Murray ultimately prevailed against Djokovic in his first Grand Slam victory at the US Open in 2012. We'll never know how much of his success can be attributed to the help he received in changing the way he viewed defeats in his mind but, as we shall see, this is the key to building resilience.

So, why is it the case that setbacks so frequently discourage us permanently from pursuing our goals?

Head science 4.1: The negativity bias

The fact is that we are simply wired to hang on to negative experiences. These can knock our confidence and discourage us from persisting towards our long-term goals. We can feel as if success is permanently out of reach and that perhaps we were never really cut out for this in the first place. While we may have any number of past examples of success that we can draw on, the likelihood is that all our attention at any given time will be on the most recent experience of rejection, frustration or irritation. Scientists call this the 'negativity bias'.

In a profile in 2011 in *Rolling Stone* of notoriously anxious comedy writer Larry David, his Seinfeld co-writer Alec Berg tells the story of David's stay in New York at the height of the popularity of his show *Curb your Enthusiasm*. When they go to the Yankee Stadium to watch a baseball game, the TV camera picks out David in the audience and projects his image on the big screen prompting a standing ovation from the entire stadium.

Leaving the stadium later that evening, David is confronted by a car driver who, as he drives by, shouts: 'Larry, you suck!' 'That's, like, literally all he heard,' Berg says.[13] David spent the ride back obsessing over that moment, running it over and over in his mind. It was as if the other 50,000 people, the ones who loved him, didn't exist. This is the negativity bias brought to life.

Why do we have this innate tendency to hang on to negative experiences? The answer lies in our evolutionary past and so we need to expand on what we said in Chapter 2 about our jerry-built brains. Physiologically, our brains are more or less identical to those of our ancestors of some 100,000 years ago in Africa, before the first successful migration that led to our species ultimately inhabiting the remainder of the world.

100,000 years is no time at all in evolutionary terms and our brain's wiring reflects our ancestral environment rather than that of the twenty-first century. That environment was fraught with danger from predators, natural threats and other humans. There was a lot to be afraid of. However, our ancestors – like us today – were not born with an innate fear of all the potential sources of harm.

It is said that we come into the world with a fear of only two things: falling and loud noises. There is certainly evidence for the former from the 'visual cliff' research done in the 1960s by psychologist Eleanor Gibson with her husband James. Toddlers placed on a table leading to a glass-covered precipice happily crawled across the table but avoided the apparent drop. There is no evidence of such an innate fear of anything else – even snakes and spiders –although we do have a predisposition to fear them (in spite of not having an innate fear of them, we do learn to be afraid of them really easily). So, all other fears are learned.

This makes sense from an evolutionary perspective. With fear so highly adaptive, we can quickly make sense of a complex world that is full of dangers. Think of two early humans strolling across the savannah and see-ing a sabre-toothed tiger walking towards them. What if one were to say to the other: 'I think I've seen one of those before. I have a feeling some-thing bad happened last time but I can't quite put my finger on it.' The likelihood is that both would become prey and thence be removed from the gene pool. Those that have evolved a visceral fear of such predators flee and survive in order to reproduce. Those are the humans that we're descended from.

You may not realise it but, as a human being, you are the perfect fear acquisition machine. We cling to memories of unpleasant experiences pre-cisely so that we can avoid them in future. You may recognise the negativ-ity bias in yourself. After a week at work in which any number of positive things may have happened, what do you find yourself ruminating over during the journey home on a Friday evening? If it's the one negative event – maybe a slight from a colleague or a delay in a project – then you're experiencing the negativity bias.

EXERCISE 4.1: MY NEGATIVITY BIAS

Write down some examples of how you cling on to negative experiences. What recent negative experiences at work or in your encounters with other people have you hung on to? How does the negativity manifest itself? Capture any mutterings from the emotional part of your brain.

It is one thing for us to experience a bit of irascibility or rumination because of the negativity bias. After all, it has supplied Larry David with an abundance of comic material. But what if the consequences are more enduring?

A deeper impact of the negativity bias is that it can cause us to avoid exposing ourselves to similar negative events in the future. In fact, the brain has a really effective technique for this. In Chapter 2, we referred to the self-limiting beliefs that the emotional part of our brain plants in our memory banks. These beliefs exist not only to prevent us from taking life-threatening risks but also from repeating lower-order negative experiences such as embarrassment or discomfort.

Why have we evolved to avoid these experiences? As with the example of the sabre-toothed tiger, this was critical in our ancestral environment where continued membership of our social group was vital for our survival and therefore getting our genes into the next generation. If we did something to cause disapproval within our social group, that made it harder to find a mate. If we did something really shameful and were excluded from our social group or ostracised, the result could well have been death.

This explains why it is so important for us to have continuous social approval, but as a survival mechanism it counts against us in the twenty-first century since it can stop us persisting in our efforts to achieve our goals. Fortunately, the latest thinking in science offers us a route through this problem.

Head science 4.2: Learned optimism

You may recognise from your own experiences the oft-repeated cycle of adversity and avoidance. This is very observable at work. Sales people, for example, often fall into displacement activity after a bout of rejection rather than persist with prospecting. Aspiring writers will often give up on receipt of their first rejection letter. Even in cases where we don't succumb to the temptation to avoid situations in which we've encountered adversity, our confidence can be diminished. This means that when we face similar situations in the future, our lack of self-belief is such that failure becomes a self-fulfilling prophecy.

Martin Seligman is the Zellerbach Family Professor of Psychology at the University of Pennsylvania and the perfect psychologist to help us cope with adversity. He has been one of the leading exponents of positive psychology, a branch of science that has chosen to emphasise the use of psychology not for treating mental illness but for increasing wellbeing, happiness and self-fulfilment.

The word 'positive' in the context of positive psychology should not be confused with its use in other areas. We are not describing here simply the maintenance of a Pollyanna-style sunny outlook – that would be empty positive thinking – but something with a real basis in science.

Seligman began his career conducting experiments on dogs that might now struggle to get passed ethics committees. He placed dogs one at a time in a box and gave them a series of electric shocks. He then used another box with a low dividing wall; on one side of the box dogs would receive electric shocks but on the other they would not. Dogs that had not been exposed to the shocks in the first box quickly leaped over the dividing wall when shocked. However, the dogs that had received the earlier shocks did not attempt to escape; they simply cowered waiting for the next shock. Seligman coined the term 'learned helplessness' to describe the despair that accompanies the belief that you cannot change the sources of your unhappiness.

Seligman's initial observations were around the relationship between clinical depression and perceived loss of control. But he then began work on the way in which we explain events – both positive and negative – to ourselves, something he called 'explanatory style' and which we will explore further after the next activity.

EXERCISE 4.2: AMBIGUOUS IMAGE

Look at the picture above. What do you see? This is what psychologists call an ambiguous image because you should be able to see two things. The first thing you should be able to see is the outline of a vase. What else can you see? You should also be able to see the faces of two people in profile.

Once you are able to see both the vase and the faces, focus for a moment on the vase. Now look at the faces. Then shift back to the vase. What physically changed on the picture itself? Nothing. You were able to shift between the two images by changing your perspective, perhaps anchoring on a different part of the picture.

This exercise tells us something very important about the way our brain works. As neuroscientist David Eagleman writes: 'Vision is active, not passive. There is more than one way for the visual system to interpret the stimulus, and so it flips back and forth between the possibilities.'[14] We assume that what we see with our eyes is an objective reality but it turns out that our brain is constantly interpreting, screening things out and making assumptions.

So if our brains do this without our awareness for something as apparently concrete as the world that we can see before our eyes, just imagine what it does when interpreting the events that we experience. The flexibility it requires in looking at a visual image in different ways is closely related to the way in which we can choose to look at events.

Before the activity, we introduced the concept of 'explanatory style'. This is the term Seligman coined to capture the way we choose to explain events to ourselves, whether good or bad. He identified three dimensions of explanatory style.

The first dimension is personal: to use an example referred to earlier, if a work project which we are involved in drifts or encounters a setback, a personal explanation might be: 'It's my fault – I didn't follow up enough on that issue.' If you recognise this instinctive assumption that whenever something does not go well you messed it up, then you are explaining the event to yourself in a negative and personal way.

The second dimension is permanent and involves time. Again, using an earlier example, if you got a rejection for your debut novel, you may explain the event to yourself as: 'I'm simply not good at writing. I'll never get a book published.' This is explaining the event in a negative and permanent way. It is also personal and it is possible for our self-talk to straddle more than one dimension at a time – be both personal and permanent.

The third and final dimension is pervasive and captures the way in which we can take one isolated negative experience and explain it to ourselves as something universal. If you received no reply to a corporate job enquiry, you may have said to yourself: 'There are no jobs out there. The whole market's dead.' As well as taking hold at an individual level, these negative beliefs can take root within entire organisations. I have heard explanations along the lines of: 'Our product is too expensive', 'Our brand is hated in France' or 'We tried that approach and it doesn't work'.

It is far better to have a positive explanatory style, although it is important to note here that we need to take responsibility for when something genuinely is our fault. As we saw in Chapter 3, we can build self-generated adversity into our growth mindset and learn from it. What is less healthy is to regard everything as out of our own control.

I have worked with sales people who have blamed their poor performance on the lack of leads or marketing collateral, the product being too expensive or the greater effectiveness of competitors. They persist with this explanatory style even when it is pointed out that some of their colleagues have delivered a stellar performance in spite of these issues.

If you have a positive explanatory style, if without being delusional you can explain negative events to yourself as not personal, not permanent and not pervasive, then Seligman describes you as an optimist. Seligman and Peter Schulman have devised a psychometric test, the Seligman Attributional Style Questionnaire (SASQ), that can measure one's level of optimism.

Interestingly, Seligman and Schulman's research into the American life insurance industry shows that new recruits into an insurance sales team scoring high on optimism outperform their less optimistic colleagues and are less likely to leave their jobs.

In this context, optimism does not mean that we believe things are going to turn out well. Nor does the science advocate a Pollyanna-ish insistence on finding a positive upside in even the most disastrous event. Optimism is to do with how we explain events to ourselves, our attributional style. When we look to develop our performance in any given field, this becomes particularly important with negative events.

If we look at sporting performance among elite athletes, this optimistic approach to negative events goes some way towards explaining success, particularly in sports where failure must be confronted frequently.

Tennis offers arguably the best example of the need to confront negativity consistently since even top players lose almost as many points as they win.

Andy Murray won the 2016 Wimbledon Men's Singles title in a one-sided straight sets defeat of Milos Raonic. And yet he won only 53 per cent of points in the match. Many a tennis match turns on one bad point or a poor line call causing a player to unravel and ultimately lose.

Roger Federer's extraordinary longevity at the top levels of the sport has been attributed by *The Daily Telegraph's* tennis writer Simon Briggs to his 'serene mental state' as much as his physical abilities. 'Adaptability, optimism and a curious lack of anxiety,' writes Briggs. 'Those are as much Federer's defining characteristics as his movement and stroke-play... he just has a unique ability to ride out anything that life throws his way.'[15]

We see examples of this optimism in other sports. Like tennis, baseball is fraught with negativity. It is said that when at bat, players lose seven times out of ten. So, as with tennis, a special way of processing negativity is needed. In *Moneyball*, Michael Lewis's depiction of how the application of statistics revolutionised the drafting of baseball players, this is how he described high performing centre fielder Lenny Dykstra: 'Lenny didn't let his mind screw him up. The physical gifts required to play pro ball were, in some ways, less extraordinary than the mental ones... "Lenny was so perfectly designed, emotionally, to play the game of baseball," said Billy [Beane, General Manager of the Oakland Athletics]. He was able to instantly forget any failure and draw strength from every success.'[16]

From Beane's description of Dykstra, it is as if the player had been spared the negativity bias altogether. Indeed, a pattern emerges of writers that have analysed elite sports performers using Seligman's language of optimism in the face of adverse events. Both writers suggest this explanatory style is fundamental to the athlete's success, possibly even to a greater extent than physical ability.

For high performers in any environment, this positive explanatory style or optimism is critical to enduring success. Without it, we become discouraged by setbacks with the result that we lose heart and ultimately give up. For athletes such as Roger Federer and Lenny Dykstra, optimism appears to be an impermeable quality.

Few of us are like this from birth, and indeed Federer himself was not in the early years of his career, as he was notorious for hurling rackets in temper tantrums as a junior. The heartening news is that optimism can be built. Just as Seligman coined the expression 'learned helplessness' he also coined 'learned optimism'.[17] In order to cultivate an optimistic explanatory style to help us bounce back from adversity, like Federer we need to learn to use a tool for that purpose.

EXERCISE 4.3: MY ADVERSITY

Think of a negative experience at work or in life, ideally one that is fairly recent and perhaps still a bit raw. It may be a bit of negative feedback from your boss, a presentation that went poorly or a job interview during which you struggled with a question. For the purposes of the rest of this chapter, and for reasons that will soon become apparent, we will refer to these types of experience as an 'adversity'.

Next, let's do some perspective-taking. I often do this with people in sales roles once they have lost a deal on which they had been pinning their hopes. The first step in perspective-taking is to imagine the worst-case outcome of the adversity. Our catastrophising Sofa-Man needs little encouragement in this exercise and is probably already imagining a downward spiral of events beginning with being fired followed by marital breakdown, unemployment and personal ruin. This is natural.

Next, let's think of the best possible outcome. This might be the prospective customer calling to admit the error of his ways and begging to do business with you after all.

The third part of the perspective-taking exercise is to examine the most likely outcome. This will take the form of an uncomfortable discussion with the boss and some hard work ahead to replace the opportunity in the pipeline.

The best-case and worst-case outcomes are usually both very unlikely. Having established the most likely outcome and finding it not too disastrous, we're now in a position to move on.

Using the Adversity worksheet (Exercise 4.4), write down your experience during your own adversity, being as specific as possible. Describe in detail what happened, in the box next to 'Adversity'.

The next part is really important. What were your beliefs in the immediate aftermath of your adversity? What was your emotional brain muttering (or even screaming)? In the box next to 'Beliefs' write down – including swear words if necessary – everything the emotional part of your brain was telling you. Categorise the beliefs into the appropriate dimension of optimism. Remember, the more raw the language with which you capture the emotional brain's mutterings, the more readily you can apply the model.

Are the beliefs personal, permanent or pervasive? It may be that some beliefs are both personal and permanent: 'You'll never cut it as a writer.' It is unlikely that your negative beliefs will cover all three boxes so complete those that reflect the explanatory style that you're hearing even if they fall into just one category.

In completing this part of the exercise, remember the tip we introduced in Chapter 2: put distance between you and your emotional brain. Rather than allow yourself to be overwhelmed by a negative belief such as 'I'll never cut it as a presenter,' say to yourself: 'My emotional brain is telling me that I'll never cut it as a presenter.' This will help you develop an ear for the negative beliefs that can be a result of adversity, while at the same time keeping a level of distance from them. The more you can feel like a neutral observer of these thoughts, the better.

Next, in the box beside 'Consequences', write down what, if anything, were the emotional consequences resulting from your beliefs. It is important here to note that emotional consequences are not a direct result of adversity, but are a result of our beliefs about the adversity. This is an important distinction. So, looking at the emotional consequences, what was your state of mind following the adversity? Did this lead to any changes in behaviour? Did you find that you stopped putting yourself forward for new jobs? Did you lose interest in the project and disengage?

Next is 'D' which stands for 'Disputation'. This means arguing with our emotional brain, challenging and pushing back on some of the negative explanations of our adversity. Was this really all about me or were there external factors at play? Is this really always going to be the case or is it just a temporary blip? Should we give up applying for jobs based just on this experience or was this a one-off, an outlier?

When it comes to our individual performance, the personal dimension is often prominent since adversity causes us to lose confidence and for self-doubt to set in. Seligman offers an interesting disputation device: 'If a drunk, reeling in the street, shouted at you, 'You always screw up! You have no talent! Quit your job!' how would you react? You wouldn't take the accusations very seriously. You'd either dismiss them out of hand and go about your business or, if they happened to strike a nerve, you'd dispute them to yourself: 'I just wrote a report that turned around our red-ink situation' or 'I was just promoted to vice-president' or 'Anyway, he doesn't know the first thing about me. He's just a drunk.'[18]

And yet when our emotional brain says these things to us, we hold on to them as true. Part of the process of disputation is to imagine that some of these negative beliefs are being shouted at you in the street by a drunk who doesn't know you.

Disputation is also about collating the evidence. You may be explaining a persistent lack of success in a commercial venture in a pervasive way – 'The whole market's dead!' – but look for evidence to the contrary. Are there others in the same market that are being successful? With a growth mindset, what can you learn from them?

Complete the 'Disputation' box, pushing back appropriately on the negative beliefs. If necessary, imagine them coming out of the mouth of a drunk in the street. It is important here to take an appropriate level of responsibility and acknowledge where your performance was a factor, but in the case of personal explanatory style, for example, be sure to make a note of what was external and outside your control.

Finally, 'E' stands for 'Energisation'. This captures the feelings that ensue from the disputation and that help you persist in the tasks you need to complete in order to meet your goals. Remember that the emotional consequences of the adversity are not inevitable and are a function of our beliefs about the adversity. By going through the disputation process, you can reframe your beliefs and reduce or eliminate any negative emotional consequences.

Now write down the actions you are going to take in order to ensure that this adversity does not discourage you. Also include in this box what you have learned and how you might approach a similar adversity differently in future.

The Adversity worksheet is a powerful tool but not one you will think of using in the immediate aftermath of a negative event. In the throes of negativity, the last thing you are likely to say to yourself is that you must complete an Adversity worksheet to help process what just happened. You will want to let your emotions settle down for a day or so before approaching what has happened dispassionately. Then, when you are aware of your rumination and if you find negative thoughts recurring, you could complete the worksheet. Electronic copies can be downloaded on the Head Start resources page of the website (www.headstartbook.com/resources). If possible, talk through your completed worksheet with a trusted colleague or a family member.

The worksheet is useful in a number of other ways. It works as a coaching tool for colleagues who may be stuck in a loop of negative explanatory style. It is useful at an organisational level to help push back on personal, permanent and pervasive beliefs that may have taken hold. If the received wisdom about a new product that was launched a year ago with limited success is that it won't sell, it may be possible to tie the belief back to one negative sales experience.

Optimistic self-talk is the way in which we stop negative events from overwhelming us and sapping our desire and enthusiasm. Using techniques such as the Adversity worksheet, it becomes possible to develop an ear for your own pessimistic self-talk and that of others. Building on the self-awareness described in Chapter 2, it is possible to develop an ear for the language used by our emotional brain when we encounter adversity.

EXERCISE 4.4: THE ADVERSITY WORKSHEET

Adversity: What has happened?	

Beliefs: What is the emotional part of my brain saying?	
Explanatory style	
Personal	
Permanent	
Pervasive	

Consequences: How could this alter my behaviour if I believe the emotional part of my brain?	

Disputation: How do I push back on these beliefs?	
Explanatory style	
Personal	
Permanent	
Pervasive	

Energisation: What can be learned from the situation?	

(With acknowledgement to Professor Martin Seligman)

Case study

Niels is a sales vice-president for a payments solutions provider based in Amsterdam. He took a junior colleague to an advanced prospect meeting fully expecting to close a major deal with a newly appointed contact, a deal that was to contribute a significant amount to his personal and team target.

At the meeting, the prospect abruptly announced that he had already appointed a competitor to take their business. Returning to the office after the short meeting, Niels sat in a meeting room with his colleague to conduct a review of the sales meeting and was so shaken by what he had just experienced that he removed his glasses and, without realising, crushed them in his hand.

What Niels had experienced was an adversity. In front of a junior colleague, to whom he is a leader and role model, he had experienced a serious competitive loss. Realising that achievement of his own target is in jeopardy, he is at once embarrassed and angry towards the prospective customer. He is now questioning his own ability to do his job and worrying about his reputation in the company. What will my senior vice-president say?

Two days after his adversity, Niels had the opportunity to reflect quietly about what had happened and spent some time with me discussing his emotional reaction using the three dimensions of optimism. He also completed the worksheet with the colleague who had joined him at the meeting.

The first thing that struck him was that he now realised that he had taken the lost deal very personally. He had also been telling himself that it was now impossible to meet his targets. So, he was explaining the adversity to himself in both a personal and permanent explanatory style.

Niels also recognised that if he allowed these explanations to take hold, he could lose confidence and stop persisting in performing key aspects of his sales role.

But when they reviewed what had happened, he and his colleague reflected that the prospect was new to the client organisation and had come from another company where he had had a long-standing relationship with their competitor. Thinking about it from the prospect's perspective, this did not reflect on Niels personally, particularly as the two had never met.

When they examined Niels's sales pipeline in detail, they agreed that there were enough opportunities to meet their targets in spite of the loss.

Under the heading of 'Energisation', Niels reflected that he could in future be more vigilant when new appointees at a prospect organisation come late to the sales process and be proactive in seeking out information about prior relationships with competitors.

Pushing back against the negativity bias

As we've seen, there is an evolutionary advantage to retaining the memories of negative events. There is none, however, for positive ones. We are genetically programmed to survive and reproduce but not, I'm afraid, to be happy. Our tendency, all other things being equal, is to focus disproportionately upon events and experiences that have caused us to experience fear, discomfort, shame or other unpleasant feelings and emotions. We need to do something about this by increasing the level of attention we pay to positive events.

EXERCISE 4.5: THE GRATITUDE LIST

The first tool at our disposal is the gratitude list. By writing a list of things for which we are grateful in our life, we can accentuate their role in our consciousness. This is a useful habit to develop on a weekly basis, writing down in a diary (or notebook) five or six things which you are grateful for. Some items, such as your life partner or family, are likely to recur. So be specific and note something about each of those things that has made you feel grateful in the last week.

▶

Do this now. Take a blank sheet of paper (or the equivalent on your phone) and list everything in your work and life for which you feel grateful. Read the list back to yourself. Are there items on there that you value but realise that you rarely think of and even take for granted?

That's because the negativity bias means that our brain gives first priority to all the bad things we observe. As much as anything else, sustaining an optimistic mindset is about what we give our attention to. This is why we talked earlier about a news fast as a way to limit the constant 24/7 flow into your consciousness of catastrophic news from broadcast media.

EXERCISE 4.6: THE SUCCESS DIARY

The second tip, writing a success diary, is worth cultivating as a daily habit, ideally at the end of the day. Make a note each day of a small number of things that have gone well. You may not emerge from each day with a clear victory, but what you can do is count as successes those examples of the work you have put in that will have contributed to ultimate success.

This might be securing an important meeting with a prospective customer or investor, or it might be rehearsing your forthcoming wedding speech with a friend and getting useful feedback. It might simply be the fact that you persisted. Small wins are easily forgotten and make way in our minds for the more memorable frustrations and setbacks. Writing a daily list will remind you just how far you have come.

Part 4: Dealing with setbacks

Action	When
• Look out for the negativity bias and catch yourself hanging on to negative experiences. Make a note in your journal when this happens. This self-awareness is half the battle in dealing with setbacks.	From now on
• When you experience adversity, remember to put distance between you and your emotional brain. 'The emotional part of my brain is saying that…'	From now on
• When you experience adversity, complete the perspective-talking exercise. Write down the worst-case outcome, the best-case outcome and then the most likely case.	From now on
• Use the Adversity worksheet when you experience adversity as a self-coaching tool to step through your explanatory style. Use evidence in your disputation.	From now on
• When you experience adversity, talk through your completed Adversity worksheet with a trusted colleague or friend.	From now on
• Argue with your own pessimistic self-talk as if these negative thoughts were being shouted at you by a drunk in the street.	From now on
• Counter the negativity bias by writing a gratitude list at the beginning of each week.	Every Monday morning
• Accentuate the positive by keeping a success diary.	Daily

For further resources go to www.headstartbook.com

Part 2

Behaviours

Chapter 5

Identifying your goals

A focus on behaviour

This book is about achieving our goals. We have spent the first four chapters looking at our beliefs because in so many ways they determine our behaviour. Now we are going to focus specifically on behaviours.

So this part is where the rubber hits the road, starting with the behaviour of goal-setting. What are your goals?

Psychologist Angela Lee Duckworth, whose views on talent we referred to in Chapter 3, points out the importance of success being about having one top-level goal in mind for a very long time.

For this next exercise we need to establish that one overarching long-term goal. Remember at the beginning I asked you to think about what would have to happen in five years' time to make you think that buying this book was a great decision. We now need to have that goal clearly established in your mind and on paper.

The goal needs to be binary – you'll know whether or not you've reached it. It doesn't need to be a five-year goal, but you do need to have a clear time horizon that should be no less than, say, three years out. Remember, we are building our abilities over a very long time. It also needs to be very specific.

Let's think of one or two examples. If you are an entrepreneur establishing yourself in a new business, the goal might be your total revenues in five or ten years' time. If you are planning a career within a large corporation, you may be setting your sights on a board-level executive role in five or ten years' time. If you are an aspiring novelist that has yet to put pen to paper, the goal might be a publishing deal for that debut novel. For the goal of building skills and a reputation about speaking in public, how about delivering a TED talk as an overarching goal?

Some of these goals may seem distant to the point of being unachievable. They should not be too hairy and audacious, in the language of Jim Collins and Jerry Porras who in 1994 in their leadership book *Built to Last* came up with the acronym BHAGs for 'Big, Hairy, Audacious Goals'.[19] That audacity is needed in large corporations where business-as–usual conservatism and even complacency often crowds out creativity. Your goal needs to be stretching but achievable over time. So, if you are an aspiring but as yet unpublished novelist, setting as a goal for yourself the award of the Nobel Prize for Literature may be too ambitious. However, getting your debut novel published is a good, albeit challenging, overarching goal.

Also, avoid confusing goals with outputs. Much of what is available in the way of self-motivational content on the internet talks about money and success being your ultimate goals. Confidence, self-belief and even happiness should be the outputs of your goal achievements rather than headline goals. This book is not a money-making scheme, but if your goals are to do with building an entrepreneurial company over a long period, its tools will help you achieve wealth as a by-product. But rather than pursue wealth directly, focus instead on building a business that can deliver real commercial value to customers as well as to you.

Head science 5.1: The science of goal-setting

Why is goal-setting important? Because a wealth of scientific evidence tells us that having a goal is so much better for performance than not having one. US psychologist Edwin Locke began researching goal-setting in the mid-1960s and, in partnership with Gary Latham, did a number of groundbreaking studies of loggers in the American South. They discovered that simply having a goal lifted the loggers' performance. Why? Because it focuses the mind and gives us something to shoot for.

Write down your overarching goal and read it back to yourself. What do you feel about it? Hopefully you feel a mixture of excitement and trepidation. If so, that's great.

So now we have replaced 'I've always wanted to...' with 'My goal is to...'

Head science 5.2: It's not all about the outcome

Once we've established our goal, is it not then just a question of exhorting ourselves to go for it? How much do we really want it?

As I mentioned in Chapter 1, social media abounds with neat quotes and aphorisms about going for goals. But I don't want you to pay too much attention to these and I particularly don't want you to plaster your office wall with motivational platitudes. Remember we said earlier that you can't artificially boost or 'hack' motivation. If it weren't true, all the people that attended motivational talks or read motivational quotes on social media would sail towards successful goal achievement.

The same holds for passion, which Angela Lee Duckworth tells us is something we need to pursue our long-term goals. Let's think for a moment about the fact that they are long term, meaning that you are likely to hold them, in Duckworth's words, 'for a very long time'.[20] So, passion – which in the context of love and desire is a hot, inflamed state of mind – should not, for the purposes of achieving our goals, be too intense. If it is, the risk is that it will burn brightly for a short while before fizzling out.

I used the phrase 'empty positive thinking' to describe non-scientific positivity that simply exhorts you to believe or think your way to success. Well, empty positive thinking abounds, particularly when it comes to achieving goals. So I'm going to ask you to steer well clear of it and stick to the science.

The science tells us that focusing too much on the single overarching goal can actually backfire. We will call this goal the 'outcome goal'. It's important to establish it as our overarching goal, but to spend too much time and energy focusing on it as an outcome will arouse Sofa-Man. Remember that Sofa-Man wants us to avoid risk. Well, to the emotional part of the brain, your outcome goal has 'risk' written all over it. So, if unchallenged, Sofa-Man will be scribbling frantically on the whiteboard some of the negative beliefs we mentioned at the beginning and more:

- I can't do that.

- That's way too ambitious.

- I'm going to fall flat on my face and look stupid.

You may have experienced some of these thoughts already. If so, be aware of them but I don't want you to pay too much attention to them at this point.

Goal-setting is an area in which sport is some way ahead of other fields. Psychologists who work with athletes recognise that focusing exclusively on outcome goals can have negative consequences because our emotional brains become too aroused and unleash all sorts of fears and anxieties. We talked in the last chapter about Andy Murray feeling the pressure of the outcome goal that the entire country had established on his behalf – being the first Briton to win the men's singles title at Wimbledon since Fred Perry in 1936.

Tennis and the pressure – particularly on young British players since Britain hosts Wimbledon – to win Grand Slams offers a neat example of why outcome goals can be unhelpful. A recent example of a British player that overcame this is Johanna Konta who as recently as 2015 was ranked no higher than 146th in the world. This made winning a Grand Slam an improbable dream. And yet two years later, she had risen to number four in the world and reached the semi-final at Wimbledon. To what did she attribute this change?

Konta herself says that there was no single epiphany or 'a-ha' moment that transformed her attitude, but over that two-year period she worked closely with a performance psychologist. One of the key shifts that she spoke of was shifting her emphasis from outcome to process and building a 'process mindset'.

This means that in her training she focuses on small process goals and in matches she focuses less on the overall outcome and more on taking each point at a time. 'I did well to stay in the present and push my level to be with hers,' she said of her win over Garbiñe Muguruza at the 2017 Miami Open. This ability to remain focused on the present is an important component of a resilient mindset to which we will return later.

 EXERCISE 5.1: SETTING PROCESS GOALS

Angela Lee Duckworth has come up with an elegant goal-mapping structure, which we are going to use and adapt for ourselves.

Turn to a blank page in your journal and draw a small ellipse at the top. In that ellipse write your outcome goal.

Next, draw two ellipses half-way down the page. Draw a line connecting each of these ellipses to your outcome goal.

Now draw four ellipses at the bottom of the page. Draw lines connecting each of the two ellipses on the bottom left of the page to the left-hand ellipse above. Do the same with the ellipses on the right-hand side of the page. You should have something that looks like this.

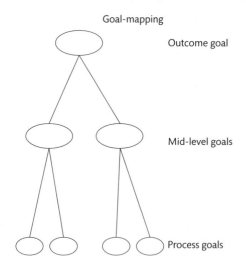

Goal-mapping

Outcome goal

Mid-level goals

Process goals

This is Angela Lee Duckworth's goal-mapping structure from her book *Grit*. We have added the language of outcome and process goals.

We already know our outcome goal. In the middle circles, identify your mid-level goals. These should be important staging posts along the way to reaching your outcome goal. If your outcome goal is to get a publishing deal for a novel, maybe your mid-level goals are to self-publish a digital novel or win a short-story competition.

For the outcome goal of achieving a revenue target for an entrepreneurial business, mid-level goals could revolve around winning a certain number of customers of a given value or achieving key distribution deals.

Finally, and most importantly, I want you to give thought to those process goals at the bottom, but at this stage I want you to leave the circles empty as we are going to explore them in more detail in a moment. To set the scene, these are the daily activities you need to complete in order to achieve your mid-level goals. By working on them steadily, you can ultimately achieve your outcome goal.

Defining your process goals is really important, which is why we need to look at them separately. To get you thinking about it, let's continue with the examples from earlier. For a novelist, a process goal might be to get up an hour early each morning and write 500 words. It may be as simple as that.

For the entrepreneurial outcome goal, process goals could revolve around approaching potential customers, for example, calling ten prospects every day and building up the sales pipeline.

Use this initial exercise as an initial draft of your outcome and mid-level goals. Only you can decide the right number of circles and the precise nature of your goals. Then return to it and draw it again. Get an A3 pad or a flipchart and write out a larger one with as many circles as you need but retain the three levels of goals and one overarching outcome goal. If you don't have a large piece of paper to hand, tape together two sheets of A4. In contrast to what I said earlier about putting up platitudes from social media up on your wall, this goal-mapping page is something I want you to put up there.

Where is your outcome goal in all this? Am I suggesting that you forget about it altogether? Certainly not. What I am suggesting is that you focus on the process goals that we are about to define and trust that you will make progress towards your outcome goal.

Our tendency to focus too heavily on our outcome goals – and cause ourselves self-destructive increases in anxiety and self-doubt – is illustrated neatly by the ancient story of an aspiring young Zen archer who was being observed in archery training alongside his peers by two renowned Zen masters. The young archer had a reputation for talent in archery, but on this occasion he appeared to be missing the target and was becoming frustrated. One Zen master turned to the other and asked what he thought might be behind the surprising lapse in performance. The Zen master smiled. 'It is his desire to win that drains him of power.'

Building our process goals

Remember Anders Ericsson from Chapter 3. He's the scientist that has spent his entire career studying the highest achievers, the elite of the elite, in a whole range of pursuits from musicianship to chess-playing to sales. The one factor that he identified that distinguished these highest achievers from the rest was nothing to do with innate ability – it was the amount of time they had spent over their careers in deliberate practice.

Head science 5.3: There's practice and there's deliberate practice

We've established our outcome goal and our mid-level goals. Before identifying our process goals, we need to dive into what Ericsson discovered about deliberate practice. There are two things that we need to remember here.

First, success is not just about investing time in your pursuit although you will, of course, need to do that. Remember that the so-called 'Ten Thousand Hour Rule' is a myth and a misinterpretation of Ericsson's work. There is no magic threshold at which you will achieve mastery but there is a causal relationship between cumulative time spent in deliberate practice and achievement.

Second, it is possible to invest time and still not succeed if your practice is not deliberate.

What does Ericsson mean by deliberate practice? He identified a number of characteristics:

- Deliberate practice exploits existing expertise in how to build skills. The chances are that whatever outcome goal you have in mind, somebody will have succeeded in identifying what works and what doesn't. This means that finding the right course, coach, tutor or mentor is critical

- Because deliberate practice involves you working on your weaknesses, it takes you outside your comfort zone and stretches you. What Ericsson found with the highest achievers in all categories was that they usually described their practice as tough and not always enjoyable.

- It involves a clear goal-setting structure. We have that.

- It involves feedback and adjustment in response to that feedback. This is where it's so important to remember what we learned about a growth mindset. This will help us reframe feedback not as negative criticism that wounds us but as something we are hungry for as it helps us build our skills.[21]

Before we get started with identifying our process goals, let's illustrate the difference between practice in the general sense and deliberate practice. The likelihood is that the outcome goal you have chosen requires intellectual or cognitive as opposed to physical achievement. While this book is not targeted at athletes, I am going to use sport (and tennis in particular) as an example to illustrate what deliberate practice is all about.

Case study

Tennis is a good example because it lends itself to deliberate practice less obviously than some other sports. Golf, for example, has a handicap system which gives every player an objective and universal measure of their ability compared to others. My former colleague Jim retired from business life and set himself an outcome goal of reaching a handicap of 12 within a year. Because tennis does not have this objective level of measurement, approaching it with a growth mindset needs a bit of thought, something that may help you identify your process goals.

▶

The lead tennis writer at *The Daily Telegraph* is Simon Briggs and he laments the lack of a growth mindset among British club players, observing that most are happy simply to turn up and play social doubles once or twice a week. Even though they consistently take part in tournaments, they give little thought to coaching or building their skills. Indeed, he could be talking about my club.

I am an arriviste to the world of tennis, taking up the sport at the advanced age of 43. Remember the story of my first joint lesson with my wife? It was quickly apparent to me that I was not blessed with much in the way of innate ability. Nevertheless, my approach has been different from that of the social players described by Briggs. I take weekly coaching from the club coach and I play a lot, mostly men's doubles.

But deliberate practice is not how I would describe what I do. I've certainly improved. I turn out for my club's fourth men's team (out of six) where we play teams from other clubs in the West Middlesex summer league. I used to be in the sixth. The fourth team plays in the tenth division (out of 12) so I would put myself towards the elite end of the bottom quartile – and that's not even all of Middlesex, just the western bit. So you are probably building a picture of a middle-aged club player who, in his early fifties, is about as good as he's going to get. And you'd probably be right if I were to leave things as they are.

So if I were to adopt a growth mindset to my tennis and believe that I can improve my skills, how might I plot my path to greatness? While a wildcard to Wimbledon is probably going to remain out of my reach, I might achieve greatness at a local level, say the veterans tournament that my club runs each September.

So let's start with my outcome goal. When Angela Lee Duckworth first published her book *Grit*, of which more shortly, I immediately completed a goal-mapping structure for my tennis. Looking at it now, there is a problem with my outcome goal (winning the men's veterans singles trophy given a personal best so far of making a semi-final and losing in straight sets).

The problem is that the competitive landscape doesn't stand still. Our club is growing and constantly recruiting new members, some of whom are very good players and in their mid-forties – which means that they can compete in the veterans' tournament (the cut-off age is 45). Also we have some great players that turn 45 and then become eligible. Because I play a part as a volunteer in growing the club's membership, I'm actually making it harder for myself to achieve my outcome goal.

So a fresh approach to goal-setting is needed. Remember my observation that tennis, unlike golf, does not have a handicap system. However, researching the sport a little further, it turns out that the Lawn Tennis Association (LTA) has player rankings. Logging into my account, it shows that I don't have a ranking as doubles matches do not contribute. But there is a ranking for men in Middlesex in the 50 to 55 age group that play in singles tournaments that does count. There are 56 of these men, in fact. They are probably all very serious players who would wipe the floor with me in singles. Which part of my brain do you think is talking now?

So my outcome goal is to get into the top half of my table. That would mean being ranked 28 or higher in my group. So I'll need to find some singles tournaments that I can enter. Again, a search on the site – using various filters – shows that there are a number of open singles tournaments for the over 50s. Perfect.

That's my outcome goal sorted. What about my mid-level goals? One might be to progress to a late round in one of the many open tournaments that I have now discovered operate in my area. Let's say a quarter-final. The other discovery I've made is that I have a rating as well as a ranking. This is the equivalent of a golf handicap. My rating is currently 9.2 and if I win some qualifying matches, I could get it shifted to 9.1. That's my second mid-level goal.

Now, let's move on to my process goals. I already get weekly coaching from the club head coach, Sami. Let's keep that as a process goal but I think I could do more with it, looking at what Anders Ericsson tells us about purposeful practice. During my last lesson, Sami filmed me serving on his phone. The result wasn't terribly attractive – how we think we look and how we really look are rarely the same – but it did bring home to me how I need to change the action of bringing back my service arm. So, while our lessons do have a purpose and we work on certain aspects of the game, we could do more to get feedback, such as have a plan for certain strokes and make video filming a regular feature.

▶

What other process goals could I have? I could play more social tennis but simply turning up to play doubles, however much time I invest in it, will not, if I take on the conclusions of Anders Ericsson, lead to great achievement. How can I build in deliberate practice beyond my weekly hour's coaching with Sami? I could do more with Sami but he isn't cheap and his diary is crammed with sessions booked by other members. I could have a hitting session with one of the junior coaches or one of our young promising juniors.

What else could I do to work hard on each stroke in a purposeful way until good habits become engrained? What if I can't get hold of a hitting partner? Well, it turns out that the club has a ball machine which is rarely used. I can set it up to fire balls to my backhand or I can use it standing at the net to get some much-needed practice for my forehand valley.

If I piece all these things together, I get a populated goal-mapping structure as in the figure earlier in this chapter.

What makes this an illuminating example is that until I began to think about improving my tennis in this way for the purposes of this book, I had no idea that I could get a rating or a ranking or that competitions existed for my stately age. Or that I could enter them. I thought improving my game simply meant continuing with my current combination of weekly coaching combined with social play. Once I approached this with a process mindset, I researched what the LTA had on its website (quite a bit, it turns out) and I began to look at opportunities such as the club's ball machine that have been there all the time but I've chosen not to exploit.

EXERCISE 5.2: PROCESS GOALS

Complete your process goals. Remember that you are looking for activities that will take you out of your comfort zone, that will give you feedback, and most importantly, are the output of experts that have figured out how to build skills in whatever pursuit you have in mind.

Do some research online. If, for example, your outcome goal is to do with creative writing, what courses can you take? Are there creative writing groups in your local area that you can join and where you can get feedback on your efforts?

What if your outcome goal is not to do with something with a structured hierarchy or progression? It may be that it is work-related such as being appointed to the C-Suite of your organisation or delivering a certain revenue target for your start-up.

Part 5: Mapping your goals

Action	When
• Identify your outcome goal and move from saying to yourself 'I've always wanted to...' to 'My goal is to...'	Now
• Complete your mid-level goals.	Now
• Construct a goal-mapping sheet and pin it to your wall in your office or somewhere visible where you work.	Now
• Complete the process goals at the bottom of your goal-mapping sheet.	Now
• Find authoritative courses or tutors that have well-established methods of helping you build your abilities.	In the near future
• Look for ways of getting feedback on your efforts.	From now on
• Find ways to be taken out of your comfort zone.	In the future

Chapter 6

Cultivating the ability to persist

Effort and talent

Remember Lee, my workshop delegate who took up the guitar, found it difficult and gave up. From Chapter 3, you may now recognise in Lee symptoms of a fixed mindset. Because he found it awkward to form chord positions with his left hand, it therefore followed that he was not cut out for guitar playing.

The combined view of social scientists who have studied achievement across a wide range of disciplines is that effort is twice as important as talent. Talent simply means that we acquire skills quickly. Effort is required first to hardwire those skills and then second to use those skills in order to achieve. Remember that when Anders Ericsson examined a number of very high achievers in a whole range of disciplines, the only differentiator he could find was the amount of time spent over their lifetimes in purposeful practice.

In this chapter we are concerned with building up our persistence muscles since this is a major component of the mental toughness that will enable us to succeed. Remember Shizuka Arakawa, the figure skater who is estimated to have fallen on her backside 20,000 times on her away to Olympic glory. She clearly had the ability to persist in spite of many setbacks.

The importance of persistence is not always welcome news for those of us that recognise in ourselves a tendency to give up when pursuits become too challenging. American crime writer George V Higgins is another example of persistence, publishing his first novel after having written 12 that he failed to get published and which he ultimately destroyed. As part of building his craft and to research the seedy world of the Boston criminal underworld and its legal system, he even changed career from journalism to law, qualifying as a defence attorney. When he finally achieved long-sought literary success, people often said to him that they too had always wanted to write. His way of responding to this was to say: 'If you haven't always been doing it, you haven't always wanted to do it.'[22]

This might sound blunt and unforgiving but it's also a fair challenge to us in those moments when we wistfully reflect that we've always wanted to do something but, for whatever reason, it never happened for us. We simply never had time or life got in the way. The brutal fact is that what often separates those who succeed in any given pursuit from those who do not is persistence.

So this chapter is about helping us understand the importance of persistence and how, in the face of setbacks, we can stick with achieving our process goals.

Head science 6.1: Why persistence can feel 'unnatural'

If all this seems tough, then it's important to acknowledge that your journey towards ultimate success is going to be tough. And to make things tougher, we're not wired for persistence. The practice of sticking at something difficult and effortful for sustained periods was described by psychiatrist Steve Peters in his 2012 TEDx talk as 'unnatural'. 'We're really built to live in a jungle,' he said, 'not society. I'm going to say go unnatural.'[23]

Again, the explanation for this lies in our ancestral past when food was scarce and conflict within and between tribes was frequent. We like to think of the hunter-gatherer lifestyle as idyllic and at one with nature, a view promoted by historians and anthropologists with a negative mindset towards modern twenty-first century society. While the exact quality of hunter-gatherer life is hotly disputed and politically charged, the 1651 description of it by Thomas Hobbes in his book *Leviathan* as 'nasty, brutish and short' is about right.

This also seems true of the few remaining hunter-gather societies that have been studied in recent years. Anthropologist Napoleon Chagnon embedded himself in the Yanomamö tribe in the Venezuelan Amazon for years at a time and conducted painstaking research into all aspects of the tribe's daily existence. From his studies he found that some 45 per cent of Yanomamö men had been directly involved in the killing of at least one person.[24] This revelation did not sit well with the Rousseau-esque 'noble savage' view of our ancestors who inhabited a beautiful Eden uncorrupted by the tarnished forces of modernity.

What does all this have to do with persistence? The nature of hunter-gatherer life was such that our ancestors might have been required at any time to go on a raid, defend against hostile enemies or embark on a risky and exhausting hunting trip due to lack of food. This meant that it was important to preserve energy during those periods when none of the above was true. In hunter-gather societies even today, men in particular often spend sustained periods doing very little. Who does this remind you of?

Sofa-Man is the source of our natural desire to do very little, to kick back on the sofa with some pizza, a beer and watch TV. After all, we've survived this far by preserving our energy and you never know when that raiding party from the next tribe along the river is going to show up. However, you always have a choice so I don't want this book to be blamed for people avoiding doing the washing-up.

Nevertheless, the fact is that we are still wired for our ancestral environment and so sustained effort such as Chris Hoy pedalling away on the turbo-bike until he falls off is, to use the description of Steve Peters, unnatural. The Lodger has all sorts of great plans for activities, career progression and high achievement. But when Sofa-Man has control of the whiteboard, he has any number of beliefs at hand to keep his flatmate sitting alone in his room in quiet resignation.

First, he scribbles up lots of fixed mindset talk. 'You don't have the talent!' is the sort of thing he'll write. If that doesn't cause The Lodger to put his dreams in the bottom drawer of his desk, Sofa-Man will also get animated each time that you face adversity – and, trust me, you will. Out will come the negative self-talk, much of it personal and permanent. 'I told you you're no good at it!' or 'You'll never make it.' He'll do this each and every time you confront adversity, jumping up to scribble something judgemental and negative on the whiteboard before flopping back down on the sofa, chewing pizza and watching TV.

Head science 6.2: Grit predicts persistence

One psychologist has conducted numerous studies in what separates people that persist from those that do not. Angela Lee Duckworth uses the word 'grit' to capture this ability. Grit is more than the ability to persist – it is the ability to persist with passion towards long-term goals. We particularly need this quality if we are to succeed in our goals given that we are going to be confronted with challenges. This is particularly the case where our goals are the sort where it is common to drop out along the way.

Her studies have included military personnel, students and timeshare sales people among others. In order to measure our propensity to persist, she has developed the 'Grit scale'. Where she has asked participants in all these areas to complete the score before embarking on their respective courses, training schedules and jobs, it has emerged that the higher the Grit score, the better the performance and the lower the likelihood of quitting.

EXERCISE 6.1: THE GRIT TEST

Let's take the Grit test right now. Answer the questions honestly in order to get the greatest value from the exercise. Don't spend too much time on any given question and don't worry about what you feel might be the right answer. Once you've answered the questions, follow the instructions to come up with your own score.

Respond to the following eight items using this scale:

1 = Not like me at all, 2 = Not much like me, 3 = Somewhat like me, 4 = Mostly like me, 5 = Very much like me

1. New ideas and projects sometimes distract me from previous ones.*

2. Setbacks don't discourage me. I don't give up easily.

3. I often set a goal but later choose to pursue a different one.*

4. I am a hard worker.

5. I have difficulty maintaining my focus on projects that take more than a few months to complete.*

6. I finish whatever I begin.

7. My interests change from year to year.*

▶

8. I am diligent. I never give up.

9. I have been obsessed with a certain idea or project for a short time but later lost interest.*

10. I have overcome setbacks to conquer an important challenge.

*Asterisked items are reverse-scored

SCORING

1. Add your score on statements with even numbers: 2, 4, 6, 8 and 10

2. Then add odd-numbered items 1, 3, 5, 7 and 9 and subtract that total from 24.

3. Add the two steps together and divide by 8.

Alternatively, if you'd like the score calculated for you, use the facility on this site: https://angeladuckworth.com/grit-scale/

Source: Angela Lee Duckworth[25]

If you want to know how you measure up compared to the general population, the closer to 2.5 your score, the less grit you have, and the nearer 5 you are, the grittier you are.

How did you get on? If you got a low score, remember to view it with a growth rather than a fixed mindset because, whatever your score, grit can be built using some of the tools in this and subsequent chapters.

How do I know that grit can be built? I first did this test when Martin Seligman (from Chapter 4) published his book *Flourish* in 2011 when Angela Lee Duckworth was part of his graduate programme at the University of Pennsylvania and just beginning to publish papers on grit. While I had completed my Masters in Organisational Behaviour the previous year, I was still new to positive psychology and had only just started to use some of its tools myself. This was reflected in my score: 3.75.

In May 2016, I was prompted to return to the score by Angela Lee Duckworth's new book titled, appropriately enough, *Grit*. My score the second time around, five years on? 4.75. This growth reflected a period in which I had used the tools of positive psychology to build my persistence muscles, particularly in growing my consulting business and selling.

When you completed the score, you will have noticed the general thrust of the questions. Look at each one again and write in your journal examples of where you have shown grit and also where you haven't.

Passion and persistence

Angela Lee Duckworth tells us that passion and persistence are the two components of grit. The Grit scale actually breaks down to give us a score for each of these.

The odd-numbered questions are to do with passion. Add up your total scores, divide by 5 and then subtract this number from 24. This is your passion score.

The even numbers are to do with persistence. Add up your total scores and divide by 5. This is your persistence score.

What if my passion score is low?

Didn't I say earlier that it doesn't help to inflame passion artificially and that you should let it build over time? Didn't I also say that passion can get in the way? If your score is very low on passion, it may be that you are spreading yourself too thinly across a number of pursuits. If, in addition to the outcome goal that you have established, you are also learning Italian, attending salsa lessons, doing an oil-painting class and taking piano lessons, it's just possible that your passion lacks focus, something to which we will return in Chapter 8.

One quality that you will need to bring to your pursuit of your outcome goal is focus. This will sadly mean giving some things up. Of the things in which you currently invest time and energy, are there some that do not contribute to your outcome goal and can be dispensed with?

How do I reconcile this need for a high score on passion with what I said at the beginning of the book about the need for passion being a myth? The passion I was referring to at the beginning was the blazing, highly emotional quality that you might observe in *X-Factor* winners on TV. Sadly, it's also observable in all those that don't get past the audition stages. When Angela Lee Duckworth refers to passion, she is thinking of a quality that is developed over time and deepened over a lifetime.

So when we think of passion as a component of grit, it is not the blazing desire that should feel akin to wanting to breathe if our head were being held under water. Rather, it's the slow-burning sort, building immersion in something that may continue to grow over a very long period.

Is persistence sometimes not the answer?

It's sometimes tempting to romanticise persistence as this ability to plough on continually in the face of whatever life throws at you. Is it possible to have too much persistence? Yes, if you find that you are not making progress towards your goals. Many entrepreneurs who ultimately fail in business persist in spite of all the financial indicators going against them. In some cases, persistence becomes a state of denial and what superficially looks like a state of resilience may actually be a lack of resilience, a lack of willingness to face up to the fact that things are simply not working and a different approach is needed.

One of the many persistence quotes that surfaces on social media from time to time is attributed to Thomas Edison, inventor of the light bulb. 'I have not failed,' he said. 'I've just found 10,000 ways that won't work.'

This is an argument not for blind persistence but for a cognitively flexible approach with a design mindset. Because what Edison did with the light bulb was respond to each failure with an adjustment in design, a new prototype. Remember right at the beginning of the book the story of Team GB's Olympic breakthrough. The underlying programme at UK Sport was called 'Success by design'.

So don't think of grit as being about blind persistence in doing the same thing doggedly ad infinitum. Instead, embracing everything we've discovered about the growth mindset, think of it as persisting in finding new prototypes and subtle changes to the design to bring us nearer to success.

Building our grit

CULTIVATING THE ABILITY TO PERSIST

Remember my own experience of building my grit after five years of persistent effort? What can you do to cultivate your own grit?

Our instinct when we think of role models for the sheer bloody-minded determination to carry on is to look to elite sports or the military. Certainly, Angela Lee Duckworth's own research took her to the United States Military Academy at West Point. Candidates for the academy have to meet stringent academic standards but it's the physical selection process that really sorts out the grittiest from the rest. A clue to the nature of the seven-week training programme is its official name – featured in the official literature, not a nickname from candidates. It's called Beast Barracks.

When Duckworth got a cohort of new entrants to Beast, she found that the grit score was a far more accurate predictor of successful completion than anything West Point had used in the past.

Examples from the military elite that push the boundaries of human endurance are inspiring at one level and we will come to more examples. But they can also be forbidding for us mere mortals. For this reason, we are going to cultivate our own grit from the bottom up.

Small steps towards a gritty personality

Angela Lee Duckworth described grit as the ability to persist with passion towards long-term goals. Part of the formula of building grit is what we've already been working on: If you cultivate a growth mindset and add optimistic self-talk, Grit will over time be an outcome. As she writes in her book *Grit*:

> 'A fixed mindset about ability leads to pessimistic
> explanations of adversity, and that, in turn, leads to both
> giving up on challenges and avoiding them in the first place.
> In contrast, a growth mindset leads to optimistic ways of
> explaining adversity, and that, in turn, leads to perseverance
> and seeking out new challenges that will ultimately make you
> even stronger'.[26]

Part 6: Cultivating the ability to persist

Action	When
• In your journal, keep an ear out for fixed mindset chatter and pessimistic explanatory style. If you hear these from your emotional brain, remember that grit is an output of a growth mindset combined with optimistic explanatory style.	From now on
• Do the Grit test and make a note of the result.	Now
• Do the test again and note any change.	One year from now
• Review your goal-mapping structure.	One year from now

Chapter 7

Learning
self-control

The importance of self-control

Remember at the beginning of the book when we talked of the reasons why we never managed to achieve our goals? Over the first six chapters, we've discovered how to move from 'I've always wanted to...' on the one hand towards 'My goal is to...' on the other.

We've also challenged some of the reasons we give ourselves for not having achieved our goals before now. Sometimes, these reasons are to do with our beliefs about our ability such as 'I'm not cut out to...' At other times, our beliefs are a result of failed attempts like 'I tried it and it didn't work.'

By building a growth mindset, developing our capacity for optimistic self-talk and constructing a goal-mapping hierarchy, you are now in a position to challenge these beliefs and replace them with new, science-based beliefs that are positive and encouraging. You also have the tools to be resilient in the face of setbacks so that you can persist.

But what if, having achieved all these great shifts in our beliefs, there is still something missing when it comes to our behaviours? What if we've set out towards achieving our goals but decide instead to binge-watch a box set on Netflix while eating a tub of ice cream? What if we've identified our process goals and know what we need to do on a daily basis but, on day one, we simply procrastinate and decide to leave it for another day?

Grit is helpful to overcome challenges that could cause us to give up. But, however gritty we are, on the way towards success we will be confronted by any number of seductive distractions, easy options and supposedly urgent tasks that we simply have to do rather than stay focused. For this we need something related to but slightly different from grit – and that is self-control.

Even with a growth mindset and an enhanced ability to bounce back from adversity, we risk being taken away from our goals. It's possible to feel gritty – only not today. Let's leave it until tomorrow when our self-control and willpower will be better. Does this make us lazy? Well, yes and no.

Head science 7.1: The brain's reward system

Remember our two flatmates, Sofa-Man and The Lodger. If you cast your mind back to Chapter 4, you'll recall that we are wired to avoid effort. This makes sense in the context of our ancestral environment as avoiding unnecessary effort helped us to preserve energy and made us more likely to survive attacks by natural predators or other humans. So Sofa-Man will find all sorts of reasons to persuade us to duck anything that might leave us drained of energy. We're better off staying where we are, on the sofa – ready for anything.

We've already seen in Chapter 3 that Sofa-Man wants to avoid risk and finds ways to put off anything that he can avoid that might have negative consequences. In our ancestral environment, this helped us survive and get our genes into the next generation. In the twenty-first century, if we are not resilient, it can make us fearful, negative and risk-averse.

We've already talked about the toughness of our ancestral environment where food was scarce and where our ancestors competed with other humans for scarce resources, including not just food but also mates. We have survived because our ancestors prevailed through hundreds and thousands of years in death-defying circumstances enduring famine, natural disaster, climate change and nomadic journeying. An evolutionary output of that experience is a reward system in the brain that encourages us to seek anything that will help us survive and reproduce.

As we mentioned in Chapter 2, the brain has a number of powerful chemicals called neurotransmitters at its disposal to help us deal with life's challenges, although they evolved with our ancestral environment in mind rather than the twenty-first century. One of these is dopamine, which I like to think of as the 'I'd really like some more of that' neurotransmitter.

When we encounter anything that might have given us an evolutionary edge in our distant past, our brain releases a squirt of dopamine which has the impact of making us want more of the same. Certain food types, ones that were vital but scarce in our ancestral environment and which are abundant today, stimulate dopamine. Fatty, salty and sweet foods in particular do this. If you've ever opened a tube of crisps and found yourself eating the whole lot in one sitting – in spite of your best intentions – then you've experienced the dopamine system at work. Foods that combine fat and sugar are doubly dopamine-inducing. The glazed dough-nut is a good example and something that tests my powers of self-discipline to the limit.

This reward system isn't limited to food types but also experiences or activities that will help in our constant quest to survive and reproduce. Obviously, we are wired to find the act of reproducing itself pleasurable and something we would like to do again. But dopamine is also stimulated by other feelings resulting from events in our ancestral environment that would have helped us attract mates: dominance over rivals, success and social approval. These are all familiar to gamblers, athletes and indeed to anybody winning a board game at home with the family.

Something else that activates the dopamine system is gossip. This word is used by evolutionary theorists not to describe banal tittle-tattle but information that could be valuable in the ancestral environment. This could be about food sources, or it could be information about people in our social group. Has someone done something shameful that means we shouldn't trust them?

As you may have observed, food, gambling and sex all have in common their relationship with addictive and compulsive behaviours. This is the result of the collision of our evolutionary reward system with modern abundance. Indeed, dopamine plays a key part in the process of addiction to hard drugs. In the TV sitcom *Peep Show*, Super-Hans memorably remarked 'This crack isn't half moreish.'

What does all this mean in our efforts to achieve our goals? It means that Sofa-Man is doubly powerful. Dopamine causes him to swell up and intimidate his flatmate. In brain-science terms, too much dopamine can flood the prefrontal cortex impairing its ability to flourish.

In this way, in addition to having a number of strategies for deterring us from risk-taking, Sofa-Man has an equally powerful set of tools at his disposal for distracting us with rewards. These rewards will take many forms, and success in achieving our goals will be to a large extent determined by our ability to not succumb to temptation.

Head science 7.2: The ability to delay gratification

Austrian-born psychologist Walter Mischel conducted a series of experiments at Stanford University in the 1960s and 1970s that have come to define this aspect of human psychology. Working with children aged four to six years old in the university's nursery, Mischel and his colleagues sat the children one at a time in an office at a small table. On the table was a plate with a marshmallow or similar sweet. Mischel told each child that he was to leave them alone in the room with the marshmallow for 15 minutes. If, when he returned to the room, the marshmallow was still there, the child would get a second marshmallow.

The choice facing each child was to either a) eat the marshmallow immediately and settle for just one or b) wait for 15 minutes and get two. Only around one third of children chose to – or were able to – hold out for 15 minutes. But those that achieved this were displaying at an early age the ability to delay gratification.

Why does this ability matter? Mischel went on to track the child participants in his experiments in subsequent years as they progressed through adolescence and into adulthood. What he found was remarkable. The ability to delay gratification turned out to be an uncannily accurate predictor of success across a number of dimensions. Those that held out for the second marshmallow became higher achievers in their educational career, getting better grades in school and going on to better performance still in higher education.

But Mischel didn't stop there. He measured a whole range of aspects of his subjects' lives as they got older including crime rates, income and even body mass index. Across all of these, those that displayed an early ability to delay gratification fared better.[27]

When I introduce this research to clients, the parents among them think immediately of their children, some expressing the urge to rush home and subject them to the test. This is tempting as this important ability seems so deterministic. However, if we approach this with a growth mindset, we will take the view that the ability to delay gratification can, like all other abilities, be built.

EXERCISE 7.1: MY MARSHMALLOWS

Before we get into strategies and tools for growing your own ability to delay gratification, let's get an understanding of our own marshmallows, particularly in the context of the goals that we've established for ourselves through our goal-mapping structure. When you think of the process goals that you identified at the end of the previous chapter, what are the rewards that Sofa-Man dangles in front of you?

For me, particularly when writing, my natural urge for gossip in an evolutionary context means that, particularly when struggling a little, I can quickly flip into a news website, my email or look on my phone at one of the various WhatsApp groups to which I belong.

Jesse Armstrong, co-writer of *Peep Show* and *Fresh Meat* once observed that when he started his writing career, he simply used a typewriter. But at some point, he said, somebody made the decision to connect the typewriter to... everything else. Using a connected computer means that you are always within a couple of clicks from the social media platforms that you use, your email and indeed everything else.

Your overarching goals may be related to your work or they could be to do with what you would like to achieve outside work. Whatever the context, write a list of your own 'marshmallows'.

Strategies for limiting procrastination and distraction

As with everything else, the ability to delay gratification can be built. Whether it's the seductive attraction of one of your marshmallows or the temptation to procrastinate and put off one of your process goals to another day, there are ways in which we can strengthen our abilities to persist.

Of course, ultimately everything is a choice and you do have the free will and human agency to override your Sofa-Man, but I would like you to look at some of the following strategies and build them into your action planning.

Head science 7.3: Purpose helps

Israeli-born behavioural economist Dan Ariely has a 'Dear Dan' feature in his regular emails to his followers. One of his correspondents asked for help in cutting down on his habit of consuming fizzy drinks. He was trying to migrate to water but, in spite of his best intentions, found that he would 'cave in to temptation by the end of the day'.

Ariely cited research into a study by Reuven Dar and colleagues conducted at Tel Aviv university in 2005 which compared the cravings for cigarettes of Orthodox Jewish smokers on weekdays with those on Saturdays. Saturday is the Jewish Sabbath, the day of rest on which it is forbidden to create fire. What is interesting about this research is that the need for a cigarette was lower on Saturdays than during the week. There was something very deep about the smokers' religious observance that meant not smoking was closely aligned with a sense of purpose. In the week, however, they had to fall back on willpower.

In the language of our brain metaphor, it's as if, for these smokers, The Lodger is in charge every Saturday and Sofa-Man knows that he has to spend the whole day sitting quietly on the sofa.

It's interesting that Ariely mentions willpower, a topic we shall come to shortly. His main point here is that the smokers were helped with their cravings because of their deeply held and long-engrained religious beliefs. In the language of our brain metaphor, it's as if The Lodger is in charge every Saturday and Sofa-Man knows that he has to spend the whole day sitting quietly on the sofa.

Do we need an equivalent religious faith to strengthen our resolve when it comes to our goals? Not necessarily. It may be that a sense of purpose will help.

Building your purpose

A sense of purpose definitely correlates with a high level of grit, something demonstrated by Angela Lee Duckworth when she asked 16,000 people to complete the Grit score and answer a series of purpose-related questions that allowed her to score their purpose. There was a clear relationship between higher purpose and higher grit.

For some of us, purpose remains something we've always wanted to discover. 'I've never quite figured out what I really want to do in life' is something I hear commonly, even among people in middle age. Some refer to this as a 'calling' as in 'I've never quite found my calling in life.'

Thinking of it as a calling suggests that it ought to simply arrive while we sit around and passively wait for it. Well, calling is an unhelpful word to use in the context of the purpose behind our outcome goal. Like creative inspiration, it's unlikely to simply turn up of its own accord. It needs to be developed.

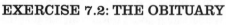

EXERCISE 7.2: THE OBITUARY

This exercise may seem a little bleak but it is highly effective in clarifying an overarching sense of purpose.

Alfred Nobel, the nineteenth century Swedish businessman and inventor of dynamite was shocked into finding his own sense of purpose. The day following the death of his brother, he opened the newspaper to find that his own obituary had been published in error. How did the paper record his life for posterity? It labelled him a 'merchant of death... who became rich by finding ways to kill more people faster than ever before'.

Taken aback, Nobel reconsidered his purpose in life. The result was a new career as a philanthropist. He ultimately left most of his estate to his Nobel

Foundation, which we know today as the body that awards prizes to those who achieve eminence in the fields of science, literature and in advancing the cause of international fraternity.

We are now going to put ourselves through the Alfred Nobel experience. This activity is in three parts.

First, take a blank piece of paper and write your obituary as it would appear today. Make it a truthful 250-word account of your life up to today and a record of your achievements.

Read your obituary back to yourself. Is anything missing? Think about how you'd really like it to read.

The second part of the exercise is to craft your imagined ideal obituary as you would like it be written in the event of your eventual passing many, many years in the future. Again, use no more than 250 words. What would you like it to say about you? What achievements would you like the obituary to include?

Review the obituary for fit with your outcome goal. If the outcome goal aligns with your purpose in life, it should have featured prominently in your fantasy obituary. If it didn't, take time to review your goals before moving on.

Finally, the third part of the exercise. If your outcome goal is accompanied by other far-reaching goals – including, for example, a late flourishing career as a rock star or an age-defying call-up to the England football team – edit your obituary to exclude anything fanciful and make it focused on your outcome goal.

I want this final version of your obituary to be something you re-read from time to time. Pin it to your wall or put it inside your notebook. This is the document to draw on for your purpose.

Willpower and self-control

What if we lack willpower? What if we're simply too tired – physically and emotionally – at the end of a working day to commit to those process goals that we set ourselves?

Psychologists have for a while believed that our willpower diminishes when we're exhausted. This is something they call ego depletion. A number of experiments measure ego depletion by getting subjects to try and hold their hand in a bucket of ice water for as long as possible before and after a period of activities that are likely to drain their energy in some way. As recently as the last year, however, the very notion of ego depletion has come under attack from within the psychology profession.

Carol Dweck, who we met in Chapter 3 with her research into fixed and growth mindsets, confirmed that ego depletion does indeed take place if you hold the belief that willpower comes and goes like other forms of energy. If, however, you don't believe this, ego depletion does not take place. As with so many other aspects of achieving success, our behaviour is in large part determined by our beliefs.

This to some extent explains the extraordinary levels of willpower exhibited by extreme achievers confronted with very tough environments. Walter Mischel, the originator of what is now known as the 'Marshmallow test' writes of:

> '... an implicit theory of willpower that is open to virtually limitless development, combined with burning goals that fuel and sustain effort and grit, and a social environment that provides inspiring models and support.'[28]

This is surely the point. Willpower is ultimately about choice and how far you are willing to go in building it. As an example, Mischel refers to Mark Owen (a pseudonym), the Navy SEAL who played a key role in the 2011 raid that killed Osama Bin Laden. Owen's determination to become a Navy SEAL burned from early childhood onwards and in his autobiography *No Easy Day*[29] he describes the extremes of cold and fatigue that he endured to make it into the Green Team, the elite of the elite.

How can we develop the never-give-up determination of a Navy SEAL? If you want to take this to extremes yourself, follow the example of Marquis Jet co-founder Jesse Itzler. He got a Navy SEAL to move into his home for a month. Itzler first met the SEAL when part of a relay team competing in a 100 mile race. The Navy SEAL was running the race on his own and finished in spite of breaking all the small bones in his feet. When the Navy SEAL was living with Itzler and his family, he challenged Jesse to do as many pull-ups as he could manage. He did eight. The SEAL refused to leave the room until he had done a hundred. It took a while – and Itzler did them one at a time with a rest after each one – but he got there.

The Navy SEALs point is that we can persist for longer than we think we can. He introduced Itzler to the 40 per cent rule. This suggests we feel ready to stop when we're really only 40 per cent done. This is known in marathon running as 'the wall' which runners hit around 40 per cent of the way through the race but often go on to complete it.

How helpful is it to look to the example of Navy SEALs and other high-profile examples of extreme endurance? At one level, it is inspiring but at another it can also serve to emphasise just how unlike these people most of us are. Social media is full of exhortations to simply persist – my favourite at the time of writing from Twitter is this one.

> 'Magic happens when you don't give up even when you want to. The Universe always loves a stubborn heart.'

At best, this is little more than empty positive thinking, and at worst it's misleading pseudoscience about universal forces. Our fundamental challenge is that the Sofa-Man inside each of us will be so alarmed at the prospect of all this unpleasant and painful effort that he will be frantically writing negative beliefs on the whiteboard: 'You are no Navy SEAL!' for example.

The fact is, you probably would not be reading this book if you'd just earned a place in the Navy SEALs Green Team. As if to make Beast Barracks at West Point look easy, the SEALs selection process is called 'Hell Week'.

Over five and a half days – during which only two hours of sleep are allowed – tasks include very challenging long-distance swims in the freezing waters of the San Diego Bay.

The selection processes for this and the West Point Beast Barracks are designed to screen out everybody who doesn't have a high pre-existing level of grit. So I'm not suggesting that you will suddenly be able to push yourself through the pain barrier and work through the night on fulfilling your ambitions. It's more likely that you're reading this book because there is something that you'd like to achieve but, for whatever reason, you've not managed to find the time, courage and so on.

Practical tools for self-control and willpower

Dan Ariely's research shows that purpose helps with willpower. What else can help us persist towards our goals and resist the temptation to stop and pick up any number of things that might distract us?

Angela Lee Duckworth and her colleagues have been researching this and have found that a tool called 'mental contrasting' helps. This tool has two halves to it. The first half involves visualising your goals. A lot of coaching tools involve visualisation and in pursuits involving movement or physical space, they can be very helpful. Brain research shows us that the parts of the brain involved in visualising say, playing the piano, are precisely the same part involved in actual playing. For athletes, visualising participation in an event – a serve at tennis, shot putt in athletics – has been demonstrated to help with achievement.

For those reading this book, outcome goals are more likely to involve cognitive rather than physical activity. You can visualise the outcome – what will it feel like to accept your Nobel Prize for Literature at the award ceremony in Oslo?

The research by Duckworth et al tells us that this sort of visualisation may be perfectly pleasant. But there is no evidence that, as an activity, it brings you any closer to achievement. What does help, however, is if you follow your visualisation of goal achievement with a similar exercise visualising whatever activity will distract or disrupt you from pursuing your goal.

Working with economically disadvantaged schoolchildren on their goals, using the example of preparing for an exam, Duckworth ran an experiment using the 'mental contrasting' technique. Mental contrasting first requires us not just to visualise a goal's achievement but how we are specifically going to get there – what our implementation intentions are. Second, we have to visualise all the things that will get in the way – what are the barriers to us actually doing the implementation?

What follows from this visualisation is an 'If-then' response. If, in pursuit of my goal, I anticipate the risk that I will be tempted to look at Facebook on my phone, then before I set to work on my goal, I will turn my phone off and put in a drawer in another room. If I feel that I am likely to stop work in the evening at home and zone out in front of the TV, then I will go to a quiet place such as the local library for a couple of hours where the temptation is not available.

For many of the strategies available to us, it helps to look back to those children in Walter Mischel's 1970s experiments that managed not to succumb to the temptation to eat that single marshmallow. When Mischel and his colleagues analysed the various approaches of the successful children, many involved doing something to remove their attention from the temptation. This included playing with items of clothing, covering their eyes – one promising high-performer in self-control simply went to sleep.

Many of your 'if-then' strategies will revolve around limiting the attention you pay to sources of distraction. We will come more to this in Chapter 8.

EXERCISE 7.3: MENTAL CONTRASTING

Take a fresh page in your journal or a fresh sheet of paper and draw two lines down the page to form three columns. In the first column, list your process goals. The 'marshmallows' that you listed in Exercise 7.1 should go in the middle column. In the column on the right will go your 'If-then' solutions, the measures you will take to minimise the risk of not completing your process goals.

Virtuous habits

If in order to achieve our goals we need to change our behaviour, then to make this happen, we need to get new habits to become engrained.

For tips in how to do this, it's interesting to hear the views of someone that does this for a living. BJ Fogg is a behavioural scientist at Stanford University who has helped a number of US consumer technology companies exploit our reward systems in order to change our behaviour.

How has behaviour changed because of this technology? An example that comes to mind for those of us who can remember life before smartphones is mealtimes. In the days when mail was exclusively of the snail variety, it was inconceivable for someone, however busy, to turn up to a social or business meal with a pile of letters that hadn't been dealt with. To start opening letters at the table at the same time as eating in company would have been regarded as unconscionably rude. And yet people do it all the time with electronic mail. It is a behaviour that is regarded as kind of rude but equally, kind of acceptable since everyone does it. What's happened here is that, for all our human agency and free choice, technology has changed our behaviour.

What device and software manufacturers have done – and what BJ Fogg helps new application developers to do – is to utilise the impact of triggers and incentives on the brain to optimum effect. Remember the dopamine system. Social media and messaging applications know that we are wired to retrieve new information, particularly where this information may be a source of social approval such as a 'like' on a Facebook post.

Fogg has developed a systematic model of behavioural change (see the figure below[30]) which plots the interplay between motivation and ease of doing. If something is easy to do – checking the phone on the table beside us – compared to remembering to bring our physical in-tray with us to the restaurant – and our motivation is high, because our brain has just received a rush of dopamine, then the likelihood is that we will act.

Our chances of acting are further increased through the use of the third component of this formula – triggers. In the case of our smartphone, triggers include any number of noises, vibrations and small red circles on our icons. So behavioural change is a combination of motivation, ability (or ease of doing) and triggers.

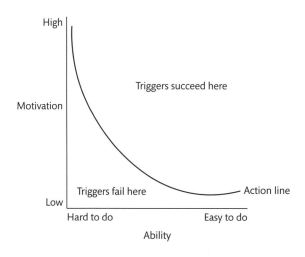

BJ Fogg's model of behavioural change

To change our behaviour in positive ways, Fogg says that it is rarely helpful to try and boost motivation. This is in line with what we have found earlier on the topic of motivation. If motivation is low, the most effective approach is to make the task as easy as possible to do. So, Fogg recommends starting with baby steps. He gives the example of flossing our teeth, something that many of us know we ought to do but fail to do consistently. The trigger here is a fairly obvious one – brushing our teeth. As for a baby step, what he says may sound ridiculous for us consistent flossers, but his suggestion is to floss just one tooth. And then congratulate ourselves. If we can do this for a week, then let's move on to doing two teeth for a week, then four. Over time, the habit becomes engrained.

Another example he gives is exercise. If motivation isn't sufficiently high to go to the gym, how about using visits to the toilet as a trigger. And as for baby steps, remember after each and every visit to the toilet to do one press-up. Then build this up to two or four. Over the course of the day, you may do a couple of dozen. Fogg himself developed a daily habit of doing around 70 press-ups each day.

His finding about triggers is that it is rarely enough to put reminders in your phone or leave post-it notes for yourself. The desired behaviour needs to be associated with an existing habit, something that is already hardwired into your behaviour and to which you can append a new activity. So after you complete a habitual task, starting with your baby steps, work on your process goal.

Successful goal accomplishment is more likely to be driven by building small but virtuous daily habits than by one superhuman burst of effort. This book was, for the most part, written in one-hour slots at 7am each morning before I began my day job running my consulting business. Your process goals may be achieved in a brief period each morning before work triggered by something as simple as having a shower or that first cup of coffee.

While I said earlier that there is little point in trying to boost motivation artificially, you can take steps to ensure that you are less dependent upon it. Are there goals that you can work on with a friend or colleague? Having a shared commitment means that you are less likely to procrastinate since it's no longer a question of the impact of doing so on yourself – you would be letting down somebody else.

I know this from my own pursuit of some of my process goals in tennis. If it looks fractionally like rain, I may decide not to go to the club and haul out the ball machine. But if I've promised my wife that we will play singles, I'm much more likely to stick with it – although even then, if I were to blow her out, I would be disappointing only one person. Yet every Saturday morning I get out of bed at 8am to play doubles with three other men. I have no motivational challenges at all with this, even if I'm tired from a late Friday night. This is because I've made an emotional contract with the others and feel obliged to turn up and not let them down. So it never even occurs to me to wriggle out of it. I get ready and go.

Finding a group or even just one friend or colleague with whom you can meet and collaborate on goals will help with your motivation and will ensure that habits become engrained. At one of my corporate clients, a number of delegates at my workshops found in common a desire to get better at presenting and speaking. They set up a monthly meeting at which they would take it in turns to present and provide one another with feed-back. If you don't have any friends or colleagues that come to mind, see if you can find established groups that welcome new members.

Creative writing is a pursuit that lends itself to this since there is an abundance of writing circles that allow members to bring pieces of work to the group and get feedback.

EXERCISE 7.4: CHANGING MY OWN BEHAVIOUR

For your process goals, particularly those that you might find challenging, when is your motivation highest? Are you, like me, a morning person? If so, plan the time that you will work on your process goals, and if necessary get up earlier each morning.

Second, find friends or buddies with whom you can meet regularly so that the work becomes habitual.

Third, give some thought to what triggers will help you sustain the habit. What are the existing daily habits that you can use as triggers? They may revolve around mealtimes or other routine behaviours such as walking the dog.

Remember I asked the question earlier as to whether or not the brain's reward system makes us naturally lazy? At the time, I wrote yes and no. Yes because we are wired to avoid risk and seek out reward and no because we can and do override any number of natural impulses that might have been unremarkable in our ancestral environment but are wholly unacceptable now. We also have a choice, always. So we can choose not to succumb to whatever urge is exciting our inner Sofa-Man.

This is ultimately about self-control in the face of innumerable temptations and distractions, however resilient and gritty we might be. We might feel mentally drained and run-down but our willpower will only do the same thing if we believe that willpower depletes in that way. If you don't believe that willpower is limited, then ego depletion does not occur. This is another example of the critical interplay between beliefs and behaviours.

After all, the brain is an organ rather than a muscle. In his article in the *Harvard Business Review* titled 'Have We Been Thinking About Willpower the Wrong Way for 30 Years?',[31] Nir Eyal refers to Michael Inzlicht, a professor of psychology at the University of Toronto. Inzlicht's belief is that 'willpower is not a finite resource but acts like an emotion. Just as we don't "run out" of joy or anger, willpower ebbs and flows based on what's happening to us and how we feel.'[32]

Is it possible to reframe our view of our own willpower and so demonstrate better self-control in pursuit of our goals? I believe so. This certainly appears to be the experience of Jesse Itzler who, as mentioned earlier, took the extreme measure of having a Navy SEAL move into his apartment with him for a month. While no slouch – Itzler is a former performing artist and highly successful entrepreneur – he recognised in himself an occasional tendency to procrastinate. His guest, by consistently pushing him harder to do more than he thought was within him, helped him to improve.

> **'Pre-SEAL I sometimes would be on the couch and not want to do whatever needed to be done and I'd be like "Fuck it," and blow it off. Procrastinate.**
>
> **I don't think like that anymore. Just get off the couch and do it is what I remind myself. SEAL would never say, "Fuck it." He'd get off the couch and do it. Regardless of the time, the temperature or how tired he was. I absorbed that just-get-it-done and there-are-no-excuses attitude.'[33]**

By choosing goals about which we are passionate and which have real meaning for us, we should reduce the need for willpower. But nevertheless, there will be points along the way where we will feel like 'blowing it off'. After all, deliberate practice should be hard and as it should focus on our weaknesses it will often be not particularly enjoyable. So accept that Sofa-Man will frequently urge you to plump for the lazy option and build your ability to plough on regardless.

So what is laziness?

If you find yourself wrestling with procrastination and find building even tiny habits a struggle, take another look at Chapter 3 and some of your beliefs. If our beliefs about ourselves are fixed and negative and if we've held them for a long time, they can be self-fulfilling. My own one was that I was no good at ball sports, but although I have to work hard to acquire skills, I feel I have put that particular self-limiting belief to rest with my tennis.

Laziness is often a self-protection mechanism that comes as part and parcel of a fixed mindset. If we regard our ability as innate, we are more likely to regard sustained effort as a bad thing, something only those without innate ability need to do. Anything that we find difficult, we immediately feel threatened by and so our natural response is to give up and lose interest. This can happen in work where we may feel we have reached a plateau in our career or in our attempts to take up new pursuits. This behaviour may come across as laziness but it is really the by-product of a fixed mindset.

There is something related to laziness but subtly different – enjoying leisure. For example, I don't think of myself as lazy but I am very attached to leisure. We do not need to regard leisure as negative if it follows sustained work on our goals or deliberate practice. Leisure is good for the creative process and for problem-solving and is good for mental recovery. The prospect of planned leisure time to follow goal completion will pacify Sofa-Man and his impulse to preserve energy. Some of what we enjoy doing when we down tools – whether it's watching TV or playing sport – fits neatly into Walter Mischel's marshmallow metaphor. Think of leisure time as the marshmallow and build your skills at delaying gratification.

Success in pursuit of long-term goals will happen, by their very nature, over many years. For the sustained effort we will need to do this, it is important not to throw ourselves at them 24/7, even where we may feel a romantic attachment to doing so. We may briefly feel that we are demonstrating 100 per cent commitment but this will be hard to sustain and we will risk burnout. In spite of what you might hear from the Hip-Hop Preacher and other purveyors of empty positive thinking, rest is an important component in reaching our goals, something argued compellingly by Alex Soojung-Kim Pang in his book *Rest: Why You Get More Done When You Work Less*.

His examples of high-achievers that build rest into their schedules fits my own anecdotal experience of highly successful entrepreneurs who consistently find the time for rest and leisure and, as we shall see in the next chapter, are rarely frenetically busy.

Part 7: Building willpower and self-control and learning not to procrastinate

Action	When
• Identify your single 'marshmallows'.	Now
• Establish your purpose by completing your obituary exercise and sticking the results where you can see them.	Now
• Complete the mental contrasting exercise, visualising each of your process goals and then the marshmallow that may prevent you accomplishing them.	Now

• Write your 'If–then' strategies for dealing with each threat to your process goals.	Now
• Using BJ Fogg's model of behavioural change, plan your activity around those times when you believe your motivation will be highest.	Now
• Seek partners and buddies to collaborate on your goals and with whom you can form a social contract.	From now on
• Identify what existing routines can act as triggers which will most successfully prompt you to begin work on your process goals.	Now

For further resources go to www.headstartbook.com

Part 3

Best practice

Chapter 8

Focus – removing time as an excuse

From beliefs and behaviours to best practice

Building a resilient mindset is as much as anything else about the beliefs we bring to the task of achieving our goals. For this reason, the first four chapters of this book were dedicated to examining and where necessary reframing our beliefs around success, our own abilities and some of the barriers we face when it comes to achieving our goals. The next three chapters looked at some of the behaviours that we need to succeed: effective goal-setting, the ability to persist and the self-control needed to avoid procrastinating.

The remaining thee chapters are about best practice: what tips and tools can help you be most effective in achieving your goals.

Our relationship with time

If not having the time to pursue your goals is what's prevented you from achieving them until now, let's look at our whole relationship with time, reframe it where necessary and draw on some practical tools so that it becomes less of a barrier. As we shall see, time is where the interplay between our beliefs and behaviours is particularly important.

For many of us, life in the twenty-first century, both at work and home, is frenetically busy. The demands of an 'always-on' culture means that work bleeds into life and our ever-present devices mean that we are constantly connected with colleagues, friends and family. Research into workers in the UK frequently concludes that we are 'overwhelmed employees' suffering from stress with ever-increasing workloads and a diminishing work–life balance.

In this environment, is it any wonder that the pursuit of long-term ambitions continually gets postponed as mental, physical and emotional energy becomes ever more depleted?

There is some truth in the picture I painted just now and it's certainly one that I recognise in the daily experience of many of the delegates I meet at organisations where I work. And yet, some of them succeed in accomplishing their goals in spite of everything I just talked about. Whenever I meet two or more sales directors together at one particular client organisation, the example of Matt always comes up. While Matt's colleagues complain about long working hours, the burden of administrative tasks and other constraints on time, he consistently exceeds his targets. And he leaves the office each day at 4pm and goes to the gym. I usually find one or more Matts at each organisation with which I work.

Whether or not your goals are work-related, we need to confront this whole area of time. It may be that your goals are to do with work or career and that the busy nature of your existing job prevents you from investing quality time in pursuing them. Equally, your goals may be outside work but your job leaves you with too little time and energy to focus on them. Alternatively, you may be a 'homemaker', too overwhelmed with the day-to-day tasks of managing a household to work on your goals. For all of the above scenarios, the ability to focus and carve time out for goal pursuit can be built.

We readily accept not having time as a reason for not having progressed with our goals, but this is as much to do with our beliefs about time as anything else. If you feel that you are too busy to achieve your goals, then this belief is likely to be self-fulfilling. In this chapter, I'm going to get you to think differently about time and how you spend it.

If, for example, you see full-time work as the primary barrier to investing time in the pursuit of your goals, then only disappointment awaits, particularly if the only solution to what appears to be an intractable problem is the distant prospect of retirement. Examples abound of people who have succeeded in achieving their goals while being in full-time work. If your overarching outcome goal is to do with creative writing, there are a number of high-profile writers who published novels while working.

George V Higgins was the novelist who said: 'If you haven't always been doing it, then you haven't always wanted to do it.' To learn more about Boston's seedy criminal underworld, he changed career from journalism to criminal law and became a working defence attorney. He wrote 12 novels while working full time, all of which were rejected. His thirteenth was accepted for publication and led to a long and flourishing writing career.

Nobel Prize-winning novelist Toni Morrison wrote her first three novels while working full time as an editor and bringing up two small children. British crime writer PD James, rather than await retirement, pursued her job as a senior civil servant until, at 60, she finally retired, staying in work because her husband was incapacitated through mental illness and unable to work. How did she get on with her writing in that period? She published her first seven novels.

While the discipline of time management can provide some useful pointers, the problem is that however much people are trained in time management techniques the same inefficiencies prevail. The answer, as we shall see, lies less in time management than mind management.

The cult of 'busy-ness'

I've been fortunate enough to meet a number of people who achieved extraordinary success, usually as entrepreneurs or corporate leaders. Social media abounds with posts that codify the success that unites such people, often entitled 'Five things successful CEOs do' or similar. These are eye-catching and will elevate the profile of the author. But there is one trait of highly successful people that I observe frequently and it rarely, if ever, features in the five-key-habits-type posts on social media. What is the trait I'm thinking of? It's not that they rarely spend any time on social media, although I suspect that that happens to be true. It's this: highly successful people are rarely frenetically busy.

This may sound counter-intuitive but a successful mindset does not require us to push ourselves to the brink of exhaustion in a crazed welter of activity. Again, this is a myth propagated extensively by motivational speakers. Eric Thomas, the Hip-Hop Preacher, in his YouTube addresses tells his audience that they are going to have to go without sleep if they are to succeed, maybe for three nights at a stretch. As we shall see, all the evidence suggests otherwise.

Paradoxical as it may sound, if you are to make progress towards your goals, you are going to need to become less busy.

This general attachment to busyness is puzzling but very pervasive in both work and life outside work. As a measure of just how attached we are, try an experiment the next time somebody asks you if you're busy. Try saying no.

If your experience is like mine, there will be an awkward silence as if you've broken the news that the family dog has just died. There is a stigma surrounding any state other than 'rushed-off-your-feet' busy.

Why? Our attachment to being busy has something to do with the way in which we have conflated activity with status, particularly at work. Companies used to be highly stratified with very clear indicators of status, particularly for senior managers. These included corner offices, personal secretaries (usually in an adjoining office of their own), marked car parking spaces and private washrooms. One of my former colleagues began his career at Landis and Gyr, known at the time as a leading manufacturer of payphones (remember them?). When he began work there in the 1970s the company had four separate dining areas for the different levels of staff.

Today, we have moved to flat, non-hierarchical organisations where CEOs sit in an open-necked shirt along with their colleagues in open-plan offices, usually writing their own emails and eating a sandwich at their desk for lunch. What distinguishes them from the rank and file? Today it is activity. For all the science that tells us what makes good leaders, many of our leaders today are pace-setters, leading from the front by taking on 24/7 work schedules and incessant global travelling. These behaviours, naturally, trickle down the organisation with the effect that everybody is remorselessly busy.

Outside work, we seem equally fixated with being busy as if life is somehow less valuable if we are not constantly chauffeuring the children to parties or sports activities, and if we ourselves are not constantly busy with something such as training for a charity bike ride or preparing for the next dinner party.

It is true that the amount of time is limited in a very concrete way to just 24 hours in a day. There is nothing we can do about that. However, we can do so much more than we possibly realise about what we do with that time.

Identifying the small number of things that matter

As someone formerly very attached to being busy, I had my epiphany in my early managerial career. I had observed that people were praised, promoted – and often directly rewarded – because they worked long hours and were perceived as someone that went the extra mile. I too worked long hours and paid more attention to my own output than I did to delegating effectively or developing the capabilities of those working for me.

My new boss was appointed from outside the industry and was not tarnished with some of the company's prevailing cultural norms. For our first one-to-one meeting, his secretary said that I should bring a proposed list of objectives for the forthcoming financial year. In an attempt to give an impression of superhuman activity and exemplary corporate diligence, I sat at my computer and typed out a long list of proposed objectives. From memory, the list (most likely in size 10 font) ran to three pages.

When I handed the list to my new boss with something of a flourish, I was unsettled to say the least by the way in which he placed it at the far end of the table without so much as a glance. There was a barely perceptible sigh before he said to me: 'Let's try a different approach. If we were to meet a year from now, what three big things would have had to have happened for us to look back and say to ourselves "That was a great year"?'

This was a radically different way of thinking but it was striking how easily I was able to come up with three very high-impact initiatives. I suggested these to my new boss. 'Those,' he said, 'are your objectives for next year.'

The outcome? I managed to pull off those three things, something that would not have happened if I'd been buried somewhere in my three-page list. As for all the other proposed objectives? Some I delegated, many of the others happened anyway without me having to invest much time to speak of. And some didn't happen at all, something that seemed to go completely unnoticed, which suggests that they can't have been very important in the first place.

Wilfredo Pareto was a nineteenth-century economist who conducted a study of wealth distribution among Londoners. His finding that 80 per cent of the wealth was in the hands of 20 per cent of the population became enshrined as Pareto's Law, the Pareto Principle or the Eighty Twenty Principle.

This principle was found to prevail in distributions other than personal wealth. For most of the twentieth century, its application was mostly in analysing the revenue distribution of companies. When they analysed their revenues, most companies discovered that something like 80 per cent of revenues were accounted for by just 20 per cent of customers. The same was true of product revenues.

Management consultants used this as an effective tool to single out high-value customers and treat them accordingly. Low-revenue products that were expensive and distracting to sustain could be pruned in the interests of efficiency and cost-cutting. See the graphic in the figure below which neatly summarises Pareto's Law.

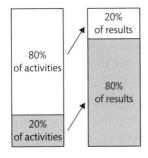

Late in the twentieth century, Pareto's Law was found to apply to personal effort, something memorably suggested by strategy consultant-turned-entrepreneur Richard Koch in his 1997 book *The Eighty Twenty Principle*. The main premise of Koch's book was that Pareto's Law applies not just to wealth or revenue distribution but to personal effort and impact too. Of all the activities that we take on – whether in a work context or outside – Pareto generally prevails. 80 per cent of our impact comes from only 20 per cent of our activities.

We forget in our attachment to being busy that much of our activity is ultimately fruitless. Also, because we are often consumed with a large volume of low-impact inactivity, we lose sight (for neurological reasons that we will come to) of the few high-impact activities that really matter. This was what my boss was driving at when he urged me to think of three things that would make the next year a great one.

EXERCISE 8.1: WHAT CAN I STOP DOING?

Let's take a pruning hook to our schedule right now. Remember the Pareto Principle and company revenue analysis? My first job as a university graduate was at the strategy consultancy co-founded by Richard Koch who also interviewed me for the job. One of my first analytical studies was a revenue distribution for a well-known double glazing company that had hundreds of products in its catalogue. The output – closer to 90:10 than 80:20 – meant a huge consolidation of the product range with enormous cost savings.

Whether your goals are work-related or not, take a look at your diary for the last month. What can you stop?

You may have identified some obvious candidates as to what you can stop doing. As Angela Lee Duckworth has observed, gritty people who succeed in achieving their goals rarely take on a large number of them, but focus intensely on one overarching one. When I first came across her work, I realised I was spreading myself too thinly when it came to sporting activity. As well as my tennis lessons, I was also a member of a boat club on the Thames and was learning to race punts (not an Olympic sport yet but taken seriously by a small number of enthusiasts, almost all of them on the Thames). This meant a motorway journey and investing a lot of time. Mastering punt racing – something still done professionally until the mid-twentieth century – is not easy and requires dedication, deliberate practice and a lot of time.

When I first read Duckworth's research, I immediately made the decision to quit punt racing and focus exclusively on tennis. Much as I love messing about in boats, the tennis club is in the next street and pursuing my goals is therefore much more practical.

In a work context, let's reframe how we think about the time we spend at work with a view to valuing our own time and questioning how it is spent.

Time spent in meetings

Meetings and conference calls are a notorious time drain but they frequently go unchallenged as there is such an acceptance of the need to be busy and so little value placed on our own time. We also like being in demand and being required to attend. But if the meetings are long and dull, or if most of the conference call attendees are on mute because they are multi-tasking (the impact of which we will come to), then isn't it time to take a fresh look?

If work calls and meetings are getting in the way of goal achievement for you, look at your diary for recurring meetings that you consistently attend without challenge. Could you delegate attendance, go to just part of the meeting or stop going altogether? If the meetings are long and fruitless, have a word with the chairperson to discuss how they can become briefer and more useful. If conference calls have become ineffective because so many attendees mute themselves and tune out, how about getting some ground rules agreed so that people focus wholly on the call?

Time spent travelling

Charles Peattie and Russell Taylor, creators of The Daily Telegraph's Alex cartoons, found their inspiration for Cyrus, Alex's workaholic American boss, in a 1980s conversation overheard in a London restaurant. At an adjacent table, a banker was heard to boast of having done so much air travel over the previous 12 months that he had spent only 92 nights in a proper bed.

What about your own travel schedule? Again, there is a conflation of status and activity going on with our attachment to business class travel, airport lounges and other trappings of the jet-setting business traveller. How many of these trips that are so draining of time and energy could be delegated or replaced by a couple of less glamorous conference calls?

So for all the romance about passion and dreams, there is a ruthless practicality needed when it comes to focus. What are the activities that you can stop doing? Some may be things that you are attached to and may bring you into contact with people whose company you enjoy. However, if they displace time and energy from pursuit of your outcome goal, then let go.

If your outcome goal is to do with life outside work and you currently see the time spent at work as a barrier, come up with a goal-setting structure for your work so that you can free up time for your non-work pursuit. Pick three outcome goals using the same question my boss posed many years ago. What three things would have to happen to make this a great year? Build your mid-level and process goals for each of the three. Then take a look at your work diary for the last month and take a red pen to anything that does not contribute to at least one of your three goals. For any activity with a red line through it, what would happen if you were to stop doing that in the future?

More delegation

Research by Daniel Goleman into what makes great leaders shows us that the most effective ones leverage their organisation really well by delegating heavily, empowering the people that work for them and coaching them to perform optimally. Among the poorest leaders are the 'pace-setters', those who have the most punishing work schedules and do everything them-selves, often failing to trust their people.[34]

In the twenty-first century cult of the perpetually busy workplace, delega-tion has become something of a lost art. If you have people working for you, create time and space by delegating as heavily as possible to them. Ensure that you are coaching them also to focus on the small number of activities that will drive success.

Where you don't have people to whom you can delegate directly, are there tasks you can outsource or are there external agencies that you can bring in to help out?

If you feel that you are poor at delegating or that it doesn't come naturally, build some goal-mapping around that. Think about what deliberate prac-tice you can use to build your skills.

What if I'm too busy outside work?

If daily life seems to squeeze out the time for the pursuit of your goals, we need to take a closer look at what you're spending your time doing. Keep a journal for a week, identifying your activities for each hour, including all leisure activity and even sleep. Look at the result and take a red pen to any entry that does not contribute directly to your goals. For everything in your diary, ask yourself how it contributed to your process goals.

Some activities you can stop doing. How much time is down for watching TV? If you have become addicted to a box set on Netflix, there is some low-hanging fruit right there. Limit your TV viewing to just one or two nights a week or at weekends. Or cut it out altogether. Build a new diary for the coming week and block the time you previously spent watching TV on pursuing your goals.

If, when you reach the appointed time that you've set for goal pursuit, you decide you simply don't have the energy and would rather watch TV instead, then this isn't about time. You've made a choice to do something else. This is where building your own self-control as described in Chapter 7 becomes important.

Also, remember the observations of BJ Fogg, the behavioural scientist we referred to in Chapter 7, that it is easier to form virtuous habits when your motivation is highest. For some of us (and that includes me) early mornings are the best part of the day for mental energy and focus. One easy way of carving out time before your day gets overtaken by events is simply to get up earlier each morning. Setting the alarm for an hour earlier gives you a sacred period of time that is likely to remain free of distractions and interruptions. As I have mentioned already, this book was mostly written in one-hour slots between 7 and 8 am on weekday mornings before I turned to my day job of running my consulting company.

Getting up early and working on your process goals is one of the most effective ways of carving out time and one that has been demonstrably successful for a number of people who have achieved their goals. Both PD James and Toni Morrison wrote their novels in early morning sessions before their children awoke. When she became a full-time writer, Morrison stuck with the early morning habit because she found it so effective.

If setting the alarm an hour early feels like too big a stretch, try BJ Fogg's 'tiny steps' approach and set it 15 minutes early. See what it feels like to immerse yourself in 15 minutes in one of your process goals. If you can stick with that for a week, try waking half an hour early. Then build it up to 45 minutes and so on.

There will also be a number of domestic tasks that simply have to be done and these can include driving children to their own activities, housework, shopping and so on. While these indeed do have to be done, ask yourself if they always have to be done by you. Can you explain to a partner or family member what your goal structure is and ask them to help out in order to free up a precious hour here and there?

Doing one thing at a time, really well

We've introduced the importance of focus in the sense of distilling what we do down to the small number of activities that will take us towards achieving our goals. There is, of course, another dimension to focus and it is the act of bringing your concentration, your full mental acuity, to the task in hand.

However, the fact is that whether at work or outside work, we rarely do bring our full mental acuity to what we're doing. Just as we have become attached in the twenty-first century to activity and busyness, we also celebrate the ability to multi-task, to juggle lots of things at once, to always be responsive and available.

Are you a good multi-tasker? If you are a worker, does your job require you to multi-task?

EXERCISE 8.2: JUST HOW GOOD AM I AT MULTI-TASKING?

I'd like to put your multi-tasking ability to the test right now using an activity based on the work of US effectiveness guru Dave Crenshaw. You'll need a blank sheet of A4 paper and a stopwatch. If you don't have a physical stopwatch to hand, use the stopwatch function on your smartphone. For reasons that will become apparent, you might want to switch your phone to airplane mode.

This activity comes in two halves.

PART ONE

a. Start the timer on your stopwatch.

b. Write in block capitals the following sentence: MULTI-TASKING MAKES YOU STUPID

c. Under each letter write a number in sequence, starting with 1. So you will write 1 under the letter 'M', 2 under the letter 'U' and so on until the end of the sentence where you will write 26 under the letter 'D.

d. Stop the timer on your stopwatch.

PART TWO

This time, follow these instructions.

a. Start the timer on your stopwatch.

b. Write the letter 'M'.

c. Under the letter 'M' write the number 1.

d. Continue writing one letter at a time, then the corresponding number beneath it. So after 'M' and 1, you will write 'U' and 2 and on until you reach 'D' and 26.

e. Stop the timer on your stopwatch.

Now, write your reflections on the exercise. Make a note of the time you took for each half. How did you feel when doing the second part? Most people that do this exercise take quite a bit longer with the second version. They also make more mistakes. When I use this exercise in workshops, delegates report that the second half of the exercise felt more mentally draining and that they felt frazzled.

What this simple exercise brings to life is that the brain can't really multi-task. We think we can, but what's really happening is that we are task switching, just as you were just now between numbers and letters and back again. Why can't we multi-task? Because the working memory of the brain is thimble-sized. Before we can commit information to long-term memory, where our capacity is much greater, we are limited to an ability to hold in our head only a very small number of things at any one time.

Tasks with little or no complexity are okay. That's why we can do the washing up and hold a conversation at the same time. Driving, for most of us once we reach a certain level of experience, is something we can do competently unconsciously and so we can listen to the radio safely while driving. But the moment that it becomes cognitively complex, such as when we need to reverse into a tight parking spot or when we realise that we're lost, the likelihood is that, if you are anything like me, you'll turn the radio off.

So, rather than multi-tasking, what the brain is doing is putting down one activity, parking it and then picking up another. Scientific research backs this up. Laboratory experiments with teams of volunteers had them do a series of puzzles, or as psychologists call them, 'cognitively complex tasks'. The multi-taskers were required to stop a puzzle before finishing and work on another, while the control group could do theirs in series, that is completing one puzzle before moving on to the next. The result? The multi-taskers took 30 per cent longer. How does that compare to your own result? They also made twice as many mistakes.

In a work context, particularly one in which we believe we simply don't have enough time, that 30 per cent is low-hanging fruit. Simply by eradicating multi-tasking, we can save enormous amounts of time. And then we have the mistakes. Whatever sort of work we do, mistakes are a further drain on time, requiring rework and often additional administrative effort to put right the downstream consequences of our error.

There is also good science on the specific impact on our effectiveness of being interrupted. When we stop our work to look at an email or deal with a phone call, it takes us 64 seconds on average to get back to the original task. 44 per cent of the time we get completely side-tracked and never go back.

At this point you may be wondering why we can't simply take a growth mindset to this area of our short-term memory. Can't we just build our abilities in this area as with everything else? I'm afraid that the answer is no. While there is evidence that we can build our abilities to develop our long-term memory – and learn techniques to store things there – there is nothing we can do about our short-term memory. Some things really are fixed.

I'm often asked if teenagers or young adults that have been habituated to multi-tasking are better at it. Maybe this is a generational thing, people often say to me. Well, research by neuroscientist Clifford Nass shows us that unlike other aspects of skill development where we can bring a growth mindset, the fundamental structure of the brain is such that you cannot build a capacity to multi-task. Teenagers are even worse at it than adults. 'The more you multi-task,' said Nass, 'the worse you get at it.'[35]

When I ask groups of delegates which of the two halves of the test most closely resembles their day-to-day working environment, they invariably pick the second part. We have to do something about this not only for the sake of our time effectiveness but also for our cognitive performance. If we were working on a car production plant where the principles of efficient, error-free or 'lean' manufacturing have been established for decades, this level of delay and error would be regarded as disastrous. But we have not taken a lean mindset to knowledge work in the twenty-first century world where our offices are the equivalent of car production lines with broken conveyor belts and random car parts strewn all over the place.

If you are pursuing goals outside a work context, think about how you work on them today. How much do you multi-task, trying to work on your goals while juggling household tasks or dipping into social media?

Distractions and interruptions

Part of our willingness to multi-task is to do with our belief systems – we feel that we are being diligent, responsive and busy when we feel we are staying on top of lots of things all at once. The other factor that fuels multi-tasking behaviour is the abundance of distractions both at work and home.

Taking work to begin with, email when used well can be a quick and effective way of communicating. However, we rarely use it well, allowing ourselves to be interrupted by each new message that hits our inbox, regardless of its status. My version of Microsoft Outlook has three different ways for a new message to grab my attention. These include a beep, an envelope flashing up on my toolbar at the bottom of my screen, a preview of the text and even the Outlook icon bouncing.

This is an example of time being something of a red herring. If I stop my work to look at an email, there is often something neurological going on here. Why do people so often check their phones when they know it is rude to do so? It's because the dopamine system that we described in Chapter 7 is stimulated by the trigger of new emails just as it is by that first bite of a glazed doughnut. If you remember when the BlackBerry first came out, the first mobile device that pushed new emails to the user and alerted you to them with a red flashing light, it changed people's behaviour. Businessmen checking their emails standing at a urinal become a common sight. It became affectionately known as the 'CrackBerry' – and with good reason, because hard drug addiction and compulsive email checking both arise in part because of the dopamine system.

But why does email stimulate our dopamine system in the same way as drugs or sweet food? Remember, anything that makes us feel good or that will help us get our genes into the next generation will cause the dopamine system to get stimulated. But email? This corresponds to what evolutionary theorists call 'gossip'.

As I mentioned in Chapter 7, gossip in this context is not idle tittle-tattle. It is information that would have been useful to us in our ancestral environment such as sources of food, changes in the leadership of our social group or that somebody in our group has done something shameful. Out brain hungers for this sort of information in the same way that it seeks out food. And guess which part of our brain is most active in this pursuit? Yes, it's Sofa-Man.

So email, instant messaging and text are all sources of distraction at work that stimulate our dopamine system. Sofa-Man becomes agitated and won't rest until he finds out what potentially important new information has arrived, which means that all the good intentions of The Lodger to get on with some focused work come to nought.

The same forces are at play with our goal pursuits in a non-work context. It's just that the interruptions may be different and will include social media updates such as notifications from Facebook or WhatsApp.

Limiting the impact of interruptions and distractions

We often accept the distracted nature of modern life as somehow inevitable. However, we are much more in control of our environment than we possibly realise. So here are some practical tips to help you remain focused on one task at a time and do it really well:

- Review your settings on email and social media for your phone and computer. Turn all forms of notification off so rather than having messages pushed to you, you can control when you choose to look at them.

- Put an out-off-office autoreply message on your work email, not just when away but all the time. Try something along the lines of 'I will not be accessing my email regularly today so for anything urgent please contact me on my mobile.' Isn't being called on your mobile also a form of interruption? Yes, but this message will act as a filter and few people will actually call. The message will also quieten down Sofa-Man who will be catastrophising about the impending disaster that's about to result from not seeing a message.

- When working in a focused way on something, exit Outlook altogether. This will make it easier to resist the temptation to simply switch into it.

- If you need access to past emails that you have stored in folders, exploit the under-used 'Work offline' function that gives you access to all of your folders but doesn't risk you being distracted by a bow wave of new messages.

- Delegate maintenance of your inbox if possible. If you have a personal assistant or secretary, have them manage incoming email, ideally dealing with them directly, delegating them to someone else, putting them in a non-urgent folder for later and, only when absolutely necessary, bringing urgent messages to your attention.

- To limit the interruptions from your phone, use the 'Do Not Disturb' function. The features differ across makes of phone but the iPhone allows calls from 'Favourites' to get through. This acts as a filter and reduces anxiety over missing calls from anyone in particular such as your partner, children or boss.

- Avoid working with your phone on silent mode and within reach, something I see many clients do in the belief that this is the nearest they can possibly get to turning their devices off. Turn your phone off and put it out of sight, ideally in a drawer in another room. This physical distance will reduce the temptation to keep checking.

For those pursuing goals in a non-work setting, it is equally important to reduce distractions and interruptions as far as possible. This means turning off notifications for all social media platforms. If your phone rings frequently, use the 'Do Not Disturb' function if supported. This means that only your favourites can get through, all other calls will go to voicemail and text messages will be silent. So if, while working on your goals, you want to remain contactable by immediate family in the event of an emergency, you can rest assured that they can reach you. This under-used filter means that Sofa-Man can be kept quiet will you go about your work.

Interval training for the brain

We've seen that elite athletes are in many ways ahead of the rest of us in figuring out how to get the best out of themselves in order to achieve a great performance.

As long ago as the 1930s, German running coach Woldemar Gerschler found a novel way of getting athletes to put in the maximum amount of intense training before fatigue set in. It turns out that this did not involve having them run up and down a track continuously for several hours. Interval training was conceived to mix bursts of intense activity with periods of rest.

At work, what we tend to do is exactly like running up and down a track all day. We work very long hours, continue working over lunch while munching a sandwich at our desk and, in all likelihood, continue to look at emails while commuting and into the evening at home.

If I said that the perfect antidote to this way of working was a tomato, you'd be forgiven for being puzzled. But the 'Pomodoro Technique', conceived by Francesco Cirillo, is a very simple tool. Using a tomato-shaped kitchen timer (pomodoro is Italian for tomato), Cirillo found that if he set it for

25 minutes and worked in a focused way on one thing until the bell rang and followed it with a five-minute break, he became much more effective. He also found that if he broke up long and complex tasks into several 'pomodoros', he would get through them much more effectively.

Science backs up the effectiveness of this approach. Anders Ericsson, whose work we mentioned in Chapter 3, found that the elite performers in a range of fields all broke up their work into sustained periods of no more than two hours followed by a break.

This also fits with the work of Walter Mischel on delayed gratification. The allure of social media updates or email fits precisely into the marshmallow model. Remember that this ability to delay gratification is not only highly predictive of success but also that it can be built. The Pomodoro Technique is the perfect way in which to build our ability to delay gratification. Knowing that we have 15 minutes at the end of our session in which to indulge ourselves in whatever is our marshmallow equivalent makes it so much easier to persist.

Find your own pomodoro

I have experimented with Cirillo's technique and settled on 45 minutes followed by a 15-minute break. This book was almost entirely written in 45-minute slots and as I write now, the timer on my iPhone is set to let me know when 45 minutes are up.

And for a break, do take an actual break. Go for a walk, read a book or, if your Sofa-Man is getting stressed at missing out on what's happening on Facebook, by all means spend 15 minutes on social media. The important thing is that it should be a complete break from work.

The more you can build your day around these blocks of time, the more effective you will be in pursuing your goals, whether at work or outside work. If your goals are related to your current job, then taking control of your diary and focusing in a single-minded way on the small number of activities that will have the most impact will help you towards goal achievement.

If you perceive your current job as a barrier to goal achievement, then eliminating multi-tasking and elevating your level of focus will free up more time and cognitive energy for your efforts outside work. If you are not at work, you can use the principles of focus – both in its sense of mental concentration but also in terms of distilling activities down to the few with the highest impact – to carve out time more effectively for goal pursuit.

For those of us in busy, open-plan offices, there is the further source of interruption and distraction from colleagues needing our help. While it is important to be a team player and help others appropriately, presence in the office needs to be proportionate. Make sure that for time carved out for goal pursuit – or in order to free up more time outside work – take yourself away from the office. Work in a coffee shop or spend a day or two a week at home. Few employers will stand in the way of this approach if you can argue that it helps with personal effectiveness.

If sustaining focused effort all day in blocks of 45 minutes is too difficult, begin with BJ Fogg's tiny steps. Try focusing for 15 minutes at a time followed by a five-minute break and do this for just an hour first thing in the morning. That's three mini-pomodoros. Then build it up from there.

Use the Pomodoro Technique to bring focused attention to the things that perhaps you currently do all day, such as email. Why not make email the focus of one pomodoro at the beginning of each day, followed by another after lunch and a third towards the end of the day? This is so much better for time efficiency and cognitive performance than being in email mode all day which, for so many of us, has become the norm.

In my work with companies, I spend a good deal of time in open-plan offices observing people at work. When at their desk, people often appear to live in their in-boxes, opening a message to remind themselves of its contents, closing it and then opening another one. It's a form of 'email jail' in which it's possible to get trapped, squandering our scarce time.

Be a time hawk

As we discovered earlier, the successful pursuit of our goals is about the interplay between our beliefs and our behaviours. Nowhere is this more important than in our attitudes to time. As we have seen with the multi-tasking exercise, time may be limited to 24 hours in a day but if we find ourselves spending 30 per cent longer because we're multi-tasking (without including the time spent fixing the consequences of all those extra mistakes), then we are ignoring some easy opportunities to ease time pressure.

Most of us are familiar with the principles of time management but few put them into practice in a consistent and disciplined way. Steven Covey popularised the 'Urgent–Important' matrix and people continue to be trained in the techniques of distinguishing between the four permutations. The fact is, the problem is not so much one of time management but one of mind management.

First, there is clarity of focus on the small number of things that make a difference. People that have this instinctively know what not to do and delegate, ignore or push back on those activities that don't contribute to their goals. My observation of people that do this really well is that they develop a mindset of near-ruthlessness about their time.

In American politics, a 'hawk' is often used to describe someone with staunch or aggressive views, particularly with regards to defence or foreign policy. They are often in favour of war. By contrast, those that take a softer line are deemed 'doves'. Donald Trump neatly fits the category of hawk. I use this metaphor not because I want to get into international politics but because I want you to think hawkishly about your time – be staunch, be intolerant of unnecessary drains on it. Have no time for dove-ish excuses.

That clarity of focus is at risk if our brain becomes distracted and over-stimulated. But, worse still, if our day-to-day standard way of operating exposes us to constant multi-tasking and if our brain is subject to repeated dopamine surges, caused by the addictive alerts of new messages, then we are limiting our own ability to deliver a great cognitive performance.

At the end of a frenzied, plate-spinning day at work, it is no wonder that we are often too tired to find the energy to pursue our goals and so we simply tell ourselves that we 'timed out'. How we manage our time is ultimately a choice, even in the face of prevailing cultural norms at our place of work. It may be that hyper-responsiveness to emails is the order of the day and that out-of-office messages are frowned upon, but few managers in my experience will push back on highly effective behaviours when they see the impact on results.

This point about being a time hawk means that you will be suitably hard on yourself when it comes to how you spend your time. You do, after all, always have a choice. Next time you hear yourself (or more specifically, you hear Sofa-Man) say that you've run out of time, you need to remind yourself of the time hawk mantra: 'I didn't run out of time. I chose to do something else.'

As for focus, think of it as bringing our full mental acuity to the small number of tasks that really matter.

Part 8: Do fewer things with better cognitive performance

Action	When
• Let go of the need to be busy.	From now on
• Identify the three big things you need to achieve in any given week.	Every Monday morning
• Eliminate multi-tasking as far as possible.	From now on
• Turn off all alerts on your devices for email and social media.	Now
• Use the Pomodoro Technique in whatever form works for you.	Daily
• Use out-of-office or other filters when not in email.	From now on
• Be a time hawk and be ruthless with your time.	From now on
• Let go of 'timing out' as an excuse and tell yourself: 'I didn't run out of time. I chose to do something else.'	From now on

Chapter 9

Think like an athlete

Taking the brain to the gym

We have already discovered that the 80-year-old discipline of interval training for track athletes is also applicable to the brain in the form of the Pomodoro Technique. How can we take this further? Is there an equivalent to taking our brain to the gym for a workout? Can our brain emerge pumped up and ripped with washboard abs?

Before we answer that, let's recap on the theme that has run through much of this book so far, the relationship (often adversarial) between the primitive, negative, emotional part of our brain (the limbic system or Sofa-Man) and the more recently developed, rational, planning part (the prefrontal cortex or The Lodger).

In the interplay between our beliefs and behaviours, our Sofa-Man will, often quite subtly, fill our head with self-limiting beliefs of the 'I don't have the (missing quality) to do that' type. This in turn will drive our behaviour so that we end up not even trying.

For an illustration of what happens when our prefrontal cortex is not flourishing, it is worth taking a look at a sad example of accidental brain injury from which the medical world learned a great deal about brain functionality. With advances in scanning technology, it is said by neuroscientists that more has been discovered about the brain in the last 20 years than in the whole history of science.

In the 1830s when a young man called Phineas Gage was working on the new railroad in Vermont in the US, these discoveries all lay in the future. Gage had quite a big role for someone in his twenties. He'd be probably described as talented by an HR department today as he led a team of men responsible for blowing up rock and mountain to clear a path for the railroad. Gage led from the front and took personal responsibility for laying the explosive. This involved a process of pouring gunpowder into a crevice in the rocks, pouring a layer of sand on top and tamping it down with a four-foot metal rod before laying the fuse.

One day, something went wrong with this process. As Gage brought the rod down on the gunpowder, it exploded. The rod shot into his head, entering it underneath his left eye and passing straight out, leaving an exit wound in the top right of his forehead. It landed several hundred feet away, covered in bits of brain and skull.

For Gage's shocked colleagues and other witnesses, it was as if a miracle had occurred. Not only was Gage not killed outright but he was conscious and sitting upright. As they rushed over to him and put him on a cart to take him to a doctor, Gage remained in control of his faculties and seemed to have lost none of his capacity for movement. The doctor, Dr Harlow, was equally amazed and pronounced it a miracle. 'Gage is cured,' he said.

In spite of the injury, Gage was keen to return to work as quickly as possible. Within a few days, however, the railroad chiefs noticed that his behaviour had changed. They asked Dr Harlow to observe him at work. This is an extract from his final report.

> 'His contractors, who regarded him as the most efficient and capable foreman in their employ previous to his injury, considered the change in his mind so marked that they could not give him his place again. He is fitful, irreverent, indulging at times in the grossest profanity (which was not previously his custom), manifesting but little deference for his fellows, impatient of his desires, at times pertinaciously obstinant, yet capricious and vacillating, devising many plans of future operation, which are no sooner arranged than they are abandoned...'

Sadly, life was irrevocably damaged for Gage who lost his job and went on to become a grisly fairground attraction before succumbing to alcohol addiction and dying in his thirties.

I use Dr Harlow's report in workshops and sometimes (not always) I hear giggles as somebody points out the resemblance between post-accidental Gage and their CEO or director. Many pace-setting, busy leaders are also prone to bouts of being sweary, often seem to lack empathy and also tend to kick off lots of new things – often causing 'initiative overload' – before ensuring earlier ones have been followed through.

The qualities that Gage – and, from time to time, our colleagues – was lacking are all functions of the prefrontal cortex: self-control, empathy and the ability to plan. Gage had an excuse – a four-foot metal rod had physically obliterated much of his cortex. But what about the rest of us? Well, it turns out that a lesser version of the Gage effect can be achieved without physical brain injury. As neuroscientist Baroness Susan Greenfield writes in her book *ID: The Quest for Meaning in the 21st Century*: 'radical mechanical damage to the brain tissue of the prefrontal cortex is not by any means necessary to make someone reckless. An imbalance of neurochemicals, such as dopamine in excess, can have the same effects.'[36]

If we spend our day in the midst of a whirlwind of interruptions and distractions in which we find ourselves constantly checking devices for new messages, our ability to sustain high levels of self-discipline and control will be diminished, just as it was for Gage. Just when we need it to be at its greatest for us to complete our goals, we will go for the easy option and procrastinate.

For this reason, limiting to a bare minimum the external forces that will stimulate our dopamine system is so important in the maintenance of a flourishing prefrontal cortex. Building a resilient mindset is not just about learning to deal with adversity and reframing our attitudes and beliefs around setbacks and challenges. It is also about managing our environment so that we do not overwhelm the brain with stimuli to such an extent that our prefrontal cortex is awash with neurochemicals and stress hormones. That might be helpful were our life in mortal danger in the jungle of our ancestral environment but is less helpful today. All the activities and tools described in Chapter 8 will help with this.

This constant struggle between the two parts of our brain never completely goes away and Sofa-Man will always come up with his negative, catastrophising thoughts, even when things are going well. If our prefrontal cortex is healthy, however, it is entirely possible to limit these mutterings to just that, mutterings from an otherwise harmless creature sitting, arms folded, on the sofa.

I have put a lot of emphasis on steering clear of any external stimulants of the brain's dopamine system as this is a gift to the Sofa-Man. Working or living in a way that constantly exposes our brain to distractions and interruptions is like handing over the key to The Lodger's bedroom and inviting Sofa-Man to lock him in. Once Sofa-Man has the run of the flat, we will find ourselves much more readily reaching for that single marshmallow – in whatever form it takes – and procrastinating or timing out when it comes to pursuing our goals.

Therefore, in addition to taking as much control over our environment as we can to avoid arming Sofa-Man with the ability to lock The Lodger in his room, we also need to build up The Lodger's ability to push back against his flatmate.

Can the prefrontal cortex be strengthened? Is it possible to build up the functionality of the brain in the same way that an athlete can build cardio-vascular fitness or muscle mass? It turns out that the answer is yes. As with so much that we have looked at, it is possible to build a flourishing pre-frontal cortex.

When we looked at building a growth mindset in Chapter 3 with an emphasis on deliberate practice, the reason that this approach works is that the brain physically changes as we learn and take on new skills, something brain scientists refer to as neuroplasticity. Deliberate practice is effective in the acquisition of motor skills such as learning a musical instrument or a golf swing because, as a task is repeated systematically, the brain forms synaptic connections between neurons. Over time, a sheath of white matter called myelin forms around these connections and the skills become 'hardwired'. As mentioned earlier, if you've ever heard the expression 'What fires together, wires together', it is this process that is being referred to.

So what if there were an exercise that we could do that would be the equivalent of a bicep curl for the prefrontal cortex? It turns out that such an exercise exists, but before we explore it I'd like you take on another activity.

EXERCISE 9.1: THE MIND AT REST

Set your smartphone to airplane mode and open the timer function. Set it to 90 seconds and when you start it I want you to sit upright in your chair with your hands on your knees and with your eyes shut. That's it.

Once the 90 seconds are up, take a blank piece of paper and make a note of what, as far as you can remember, your thoughts were during the activity.

The chances were that, for the duration of the 90 seconds, your thoughts were a random mess of whatever happens to be on your mind at the moment, including what shopping you need to pick up from the supermarket, whose call you haven't returned and anything else. If you have any particular worries on your mind, these may have also surfaced in some form during the activity. If you felt your mind racing around between any of the above then rest assured that this is pretty normal.

When Sofa-Man is agitated, two types of negative thought recur in particular, those focusing on the past and those on the future. Dwelling on things that have happened in the past is called 'rumination' by psychologists. Remember the survival mechanism we described in Chapter 4? Because we do not come into the world knowing what to fear, we learn our fears through negative experiences. When this process works healthily, we retain an unpleasant memory of a bad experience and this helps us to remember to avoid it in the future. Most of us in the developed world have had such untroubled lives that we can struggle to see this process in action overtly in our own experience. My disastrous schoolboy encounter with gin (not something I plan to elaborate on here) means that even a slight whiff makes me feel nauseous – even more than 30 years after the event. Many people I speak to have one spirit with which they have a similarly enduring recall to adolescent excess.

However, this survival mechanism can work unhealthily, particularly if we ruminate to excess, dwelling on a negative event to the extent that the same negative thoughts recur, possibly to the point of preventing us sleeping properly.

The other type of negative thought concerns the future. It is increasingly understood that one of the most important attributes of the human mind is its ability to run scenarios about the future. Unlike language, which exists to some extent in other mammals, this is what makes humans unique. As Martin Seligman said when he spoke in London in 2016, 'A monkey can pick up a stick and use it to get termites out of a mound; what it can't do is plan to do it tomorrow.' Once you start to develop a sense of awareness of your own mental chatter, you will understand that we do this all the time. It often takes the form of fantasising or daydreaming. When we do this negatively because we are worried about how things are going to turn out, then this becomes catastrophising.

Both ruminating and catastrophising are functions of an over-reaching limbic system. For mentally healthy people, the tools of learned optimism can be very helpful in managing them. Where levels of anxiety reach a level that threatens mental health, then clinical intervention may be needed. Not being a clinical psychologist, I don't propose to cover that here, but it is worth observing that some effective talking therapies such as cognitive behavioural therapy are based on the same principles as learned optimism.

There is another intervention that is widely used both by clinicians and by performance coaches. Mindfulness. You may have come across this in recent years as it has received a good deal of coverage in the press and media. You may even have tried it. If you did give it a try but didn't stick with it (or if you simply dismissed it as yet another New Age fad) I would like you to give it another go as part of your plan.

You may also have come across mindfulness in the context of Buddhism where it is more frequently referred to as meditation. The two are very similar but I will refer just to mindfulness as we will be looking at it purely in a secular context.

When you read that I am recommending mindfulness, you may be asking yourself how this fits in with everything I've said about scientific evidence and the need to avoid pseudoscience. Well, mindfulness does indeed have its roots in Buddhist practice going back as far as 3,000 years. Nevertheless, it is a good example of how the scientific process can be really helpful in building an evidence base in order to demonstrate the validity of ancient practices.

Mindfulness is an outstanding example of the openness of science to potential interventions that do not have their origins in recent times. Just as many alternative therapies – homeopathy is a prominent example – have been found to have no benefit, there is now a wealth of scientific evidence that mindfulness does have proven benefits, from the reduction of anxiety to improved focus and cognitive flexibility.

Head science 9.1: What is mindfulness?

Mindfulness exists on many levels but there are two that are important for us right now. First, as a continuous state of mind, it refers to our ability to be present, to be in the moment, without judgement. This manifests itself in the way we engage fully with whatever we are doing (see the fit with what we discussed in Chapter 8), in the way that we listen intently to whoever we are with and even the way we eat (mindful eating is something that I have yet to master).

We are going to focus on its second dimension which is as a practice, something we do for cognitive performance each day in the same way that an elite athlete might begin each day with a workout at the gym.

EXERCISE 9.2: MINDFULNESS IN PRACTICE

We are now going to do a very simple exercise which, while not being a proper mindfulness exercise, will give you some idea of the experience.

Switch your phone to airplane mode so you are not disturbed and set the timer for five minutes.

As with the exercise earlier in this chapter, you are going to sit upright for the whole five minutes with your eyes shut, breathing in and out through your nose. Breathe naturally and don't impose any particular rhythm to your breath. As you breathe, count 'One' silently in your head on the in-breath and then 'Two' as you exhale. Continue with three on the next in-breath and so on until you reach ten, at which point return to one.

Try to focus exclusively on your breath as it goes in and out. Some people like to note the sensation of the rising and falling diaphragm or the air on the end of their nose.

As you get distracted by other thoughts (and you will), gently bring the focus each time back to the breath and continue counting. Do this without getting frustrated with yourself or judgemental about the thoughts.

Any number of things may happen as you do this exercise. It's just possible that you will fall asleep. If you find yourself so distracted by other thoughts that it becomes impossible to count your breath, do persist until the end of the five minutes since, as we shall see, that experience is partly the point.

Once you've completed the exercise, make a note of your thoughts. Did you succeed, even briefly, in keeping your thought focused on the breath? What happened with your thoughts? Were they racing about all over the place like a labrador that's suddenly been let off the leash in a park? Did you find your mind drawn to any particular past or future issues?

Each time that you found that your thoughts had wandered during the exercise, your mental action in returning your focus back to the breath was a little like doing a bicep curl for your prefrontal cortex. This ability to be in the present moment and to sustain our attention on it without catastrophising about the future or ruminating over the past is central to the cognitive performance we looked at in the last chapter. And the practice of mindfulness builds it just as going to the gym can build muscle tone or cardiovascular fitness.

Head science 9.2: The neurology of mindfulness

So what is actually going on here with the brain? Many scientists have written compellingly about the neurology of mindfulness and among the best writing is that of neuropsychologist Rick Hanson and neurologist Richard Mendius in their book *Buddha's Brain*. Here's what they say about using mindfulness to improve focus:

'No matter where you start, you can become better at
concentration. It's like a muscle: when you use it, it gets
stronger.'[37]

Those that practice mindfulness over many, many years report a sustained
level of presence which fuels a sense of equanimity. I can personally vouch
for this as a lasting benefit but scientific evidence supports this as expert
mindfulness practitioners have been observed under FMRi scanners.

As Hanson and Mendius write, this state of equanimity 'is probably associated with the high-frequency gamma waves that are seen in experienced
meditators. As a person goes deeper into meditation, there appears to be
both a spreading and a strengthening of gamma wave activity, which pre-
sumably underlies the experience of a growing spaciousness and stability
of awareness.'[38]

The feeling described here is probably akin to what elite athletes feel at
key points in their performance when they talk of being 'in the zone'. Many
top sports performers such as Novak Djokovic practise mindfulness regularly in order to help them get to and stay in the zone.

Mindfulness is an important component of our plan as it effectively beefs
up The Lodger and makes him much more able to keep control of Sofa-
Man. Sofa-Man's negative mutterings will never go away altogether, but with
a consistent mindfulness practice they will become quieter and quieter as
Sofa-Man learns to sit with his arms folded as you pursue your goals. Every
function of the prefrontal cortex that we have described in this book –
from delaying gratification, to focus, to managing negative thoughts and
sustaining a growth mindset – is strengthened as a result of mindfulness.

Building your own mindfulness practice

There is an abundance of websites and apps to help with a guided mindfulness practice. The first step is for you to build it into your existing plans for
goal pursuit. I recommend finding a time and place where you are least
likely to be disturbed and, according to the habit-forming science of BJ
Fogg, when your motivation is likely to be highest.

For most people, including me, this means carving out time first thing in the morning. My preference is to find ten minutes after exercise and a shower but before breakfast. I have experimented with going straight into mindfulness on waking but found I got more out of the practice when my mind had an opportunity to warm up for a while.

You may find it helpful to use an online audio recording of a guided meditation to start with. If you succeed in persisting with the practice, you will find that you no longer need the recording as a guide. As a starting point, I recommend Jon Kabat-Zinn, one of the world's leading exponents of mindfulness. He is founder of the Stress Reduction Clinic at the University of Massachusetts Medical Center. His ten-minute guided mindfulness session can be found here: www.youtube.com/watch?v=8HYLyuJZKno

Some of the language in Kabat-Zinn's session may at first seem New Age or too soft and fluffy but I would urge you to stay with it and trust that the practice has a solid evidence base behind it to attest to its efficacy.

Mindfulness takes persistence and it may take as long as six or eight weeks before you notice any change to your mental equanimity or your ability to focus. If your experience is anything like my own, you will see benefits above and beyond the ability to focus on your goals. I noticed a very welcome decline in emotional reactivity and irascibility, something that was particularly appreciated by those around me. Even so, there still remains the occasional morning in which I am distracted for no apparent reason and sustaining attention on the breath feels impossible. The key is to accept your state of mind each day, whatever it is, and persist.

Part 9: Take your prefrontal cortex to the gym

Action	When
• Plan a daily ten-minute mindfulness session in your schedule, ideally first thing in the morning.	Daily
• Make a note in your journal of your experience, noting what thoughts might be distracting you from focus on the breath.	Daily
• Make a note of any general changes in your temperament or behaviour as a result of your mindfulness practice.	From now on

Chapter **10**

The virtuous habits of high performance

The marginal gains approach

Elite athletes invest time not only in physical fitness and the skills and techniques of their discipline. They also work on and get support in almost every surrounding aspect of their lives.

British Cycling, and in particular its performance director Sir Dave Brailsford, is well-known for the mantra of 'the aggregation of marginal gains' in which the cumulative impact of a number of tiny improvements can make all the difference between winning and losing. The Tour de France may be competed over many days and stages but the margin of victory is surprisingly tiny. Chris Froome's fourth victory in 2017 was by just 54 seconds, absolutely tiny if expressed as a percentage of the elapsed time of the whole competition – 0.02 per cent of the total time of 86 hours, 20 minutes and 55 seconds.

Successive Tour de France victories by British riders after such a long period in which a Briton had never won are in part down to this marginal gains approach. Every dimension of the cyclist's life was examined in minutiae to see if it could yield even the smallest competitive advantage.

For warming up at each stage, stationary turbo-bikes were brought to the start point, something that was felt to be ridiculous by other teams at first but which is now universally copied.

A prominent example was to look at the importance of sleep in the cyclist's performance. In order to ensure that no effort was spared in helping the athletes get a good night's sleep, their individual bedding was taken to each of the 21 hotels at which they stayed during the tour.

What aspects of your everyday life can be changed to help you in support of goal pursuit?

A good night's sleep

Just as with Chris Froome on the Tour de France, so for you in pursuit of your goals it is essential, for all the YouTube exhortations of the Hip-Hop Preacher and other motivational speakers, to get a good night's sleep. Since your outcome goals are likely to require a high level of cognitive performance, it is arguable that sleep is more important to you than to an elite athlete.

Sadly, our always-on culture in the twenty-first century often gets in the way of good quality sleep. Part of our attachment to busyness means that we often remain connected to our work or social networks well into the evening and even through the night. As we saw in Chapter 8, our devices, apps and networks all deliberately exploit our brain's dopamine system to give us a powerful neurological urge to check new messages and notifications. Anecdotally, I come across many people that sleep with their phones by their bedside table and check new emails as they arrive through the night.

The science tells us that short-changing ourselves on sleep is a poor idea. Charles Czeisler is the Director of the Division of Sleep Medicine at the Harvard Medical School and has spent over three decades researching the relationship between sleep and the physiology of the human circadian clock. His research has established clearly the negative impacts of the lack of sleep on cognitive performance. Going without sleep for 18 consecutive hours will be detrimental to reaction speed, both short- and long-term memory, ability to focus, decision-making capacity, cognitive speed and spatial orientation. If we limit our nightly sleep allowance to less than six hours for several consecutive nights, then a sleep deficit will multiply these factors.

In an interview in the October 2006 edition of the *Harvard Business Review*, Czeisler describes the machismo 'always-on' work culture that equates sleeplessness with high performance as akin to the bygone era in which men that could hold their drink were celebrated.

> **'It amazes me that contemporary work and social culture glorifies sleeplessness in the way we once glorified people who could hold their liquor. We now know that 24 hours without sleep or a week of sleeping four or five hours a night induces an impairment equivalent to a blood alcohol level of 0.1 per cent. We would never say, "This person is a great worker! He's drunk all the time!" yet we continue to celebrate people who sacrifice sleep.'[39]**

Great sleep is not just about preventing the negative impacts of sleeplessness. It is also increasingly understood that it helps with important processes such as creativity and problem-solving. Short naps are also proven to help with creativity in particular and have been favoured by writers and artists for centuries.

Just as we need to avoid interruptions and distractions when we are working on our goals, so we need to do so with sleep to ensure that as much of it as possible is rapid eye-movement or REM sleep, since this is where physical recovery takes place. As we get older, we are already likely to be faced with more disruption. After the age of 40, our sleep becomes more fragmented as we are more sensitive to noise, our own increasing bodily aches and pains and the onset of sleep disorders such as apnoea, when breathing briefly ceases, causing us to wake up.

Here are some tips for better sleep:

- Avoid caffeine after 1pm. Caffeine has a half-life of around nine hours so drinking it late in the day is likely to inhibit sleep or the amount of time spent in REM. This applies most obviously to coffee and tea but also to caffeinated soft drinks.

- Do not have electronic devices in the bedroom. If you use your phone as an alarm, turn it to airplane or do not disturb mode.

- Avoid all electronic devices that emit blue light for two hours before bedtime. This has been shown to tamper with the body's creation of melatonin with negative impact on our circadian rhythms. Kindle devices do not emit blue light and are an exception. (If you have a Kindle Fire, however, use it solely for reading and resist the temptation to surf or check email).

- Get outside for a walk at some point during the day, ideally around the middle of the day. A short spell of natural light at this point has been shown to help us get to sleep at night.

- If ruminating over recent events or worries about present issues prevents you from falling asleep – or inhibits you from getting back to sleep if you wake up during the night – use mindfulness to help you.

A healthy diet

Diet is a hugely complex part of our health and wellbeing and one where science is making new discoveries daily. Just in terms of cognitive performance there are a few things that can help.

We've mentioned caffeine in the context of sleep where its half-life can be a barrier to good sleep. Nevertheless, there is evidence that caffeine does help with focus and alertness so some good coffee first thing in the morning is by no means a bad thing.

What might surprise you is that nicotine is also proven to help with cognitive performance. This does not mean that I am advocating smoking by any means since scientific research has established that there is no safe minimum level for cigarette smoking. However, some writers such as 'bio-hacker' Dave Asprey recommend the use by non-smokers of nicotine gum or patches to boost cognitive performance, citing some recent research as to its efficacy. Personally, this is not something I have pursued not least because nicotine is addictive and, as Asprey himself points out, stimulates the dopamine system, something we should be at pains to avoid.

When mental energy is low, it is tempting to reach for foods that may give us a temporary boost, particularly something sweet. This should be avoided not least because the short boost will be followed in short order by an energy crash. Furthermore, the spike in insulin resistance means that the body will then crave more sugary foods.

Carbohydrates, particularly of the refined type in snacks and bread, also have a similar if slightly less direct impact. Refined carbs are converted by the body into starch which then gets quickly converted to sugar. Just as our wiring has not changed since our evolutionary past, so too with our digestive system which did not evolve for an abundance of refined sugars and carbohydrates. This is why many diets advocate eating what would have been natural for our ancestors in their environment: protein in the form of meat and fish, fruit, nuts, vegetables, pulses, seeds and berries.

Our ancestral diet would also have included a good deal of fat – subject to availability – something that has had a bad press for several decades now and has been painted as a villain and the cause of common modern ailments such as heart disease and obesity. Fat and cholesterol are rapidly being reappraised, particularly as their importance to brain health may turn out to be greater than previously thought.

If you are depressed by the avoidance of refined sugars and carbs, you may like Asprey's advocacy of dark chocolate since it is full of polyphenols, something he describes as brain-boosting antioxidants. However, he recommends at least 85 per cent cocoa solids.

As for drink, sugary drinks fall into the same category as foods with refined sugars. In diet drinks, artificial sweeteners such as aspartame are not good for cognitive performance as well as being poor for health in general. Asprey has found that it is 'known as an excitatory neurotoxin because it causes your synapses to fire repeatedly... Your neurons are full of mitochondria [organs within brain cells critically responsible for creating energy] because firing takes up so much energy. When your neurons fire relentlessly because you ate a man-made chemical, you're taxing your mitochondria at the exact same time that you're poisoning them.'[40]

As for other non-alcoholic drinks, fruit juices lack the fibre of the fruit itself but are very high in fructose, the sugar contained naturally in fruit, which should be avoided for the same reasons as sugar in other forms.

We are often advised to stay hydrated and drink lots of water. In a 2010 study on hydration, a UK Nutrition Council report concluded that this advice is often overplayed since our natural thirst reflex is a pretty effective and well-established device the body has for letting us know that we need to take a drink. Among the myths it identifies surrounding water are the requirement for two litres a day. Not only is there no scientific basis for this but nobody can identify where this suggestion originated. Also, we do not need to drink lots of water to detoxify since, again, our body is pretty good at doing this whatever our levels of hydration.

As for the role of hydration in cognitive performance, laboratory research has explored this by having two teams complete a series of 'cognitively complex tasks' (puzzles to the rest of us). One team acted as a control group and could drink as much water as desired while the other was denied water. The performance in completing the puzzles was used as a measure of cognitive impairment. No impairment was identifiable in the second team until its members were so dehydrated that they had lost 2 per cent of their body weight. By this time, of course, they were also completely parched and, were it not for the experiment, would have been drinking water in any case.

So, in answer to the question of staying hydrated, have something to drink when you're thirsty.

Here are some tips on diet:

- Avoid food and drink that will cause spikes – and then troughs – in energy such as those containing sugar and refined carbohydrates.

- Snack on berries and nuts when peckish.

- Drink coffee in the mornings for alertness and mental energy.

- Consider science-based diets that reflect our evolutionary past.

The importance of exercise

Exercise supports not just physical health but cognitive performance also. It helps with sleep and improves the creative process.

Research into the impact of exercise on the brain shows that much in the same way that cardiovascular workouts improve the health of the heart and lungs, so exercise can also improve the structure and health of the brain. What do I mean by structure? Research in 2015 showed that exercise 'induces profound structural brain plasticity'. The creation of new neurons is stimulated by exercise and running especially has been shown to be conducive to neurogenesis.

This may go some way to explaining how exercise seems to support the creative process. As well as neurologically supporting brain growth, occupying ourselves in something outside the pursuit of our goals can have surprisingly beneficial results. When we think that our brain is doing nothing – such as when we are on a run or just at rest – it is surprisingly active. The brain's default mode network, a series of interconnected parts of the brain, is switched on and becomes just as busy on 'internal' cognitive tasks as other parts of the brain were previously when engaged on external ones.

This explains why sometimes problems get solved or new ideas arrive most readily when we are away from our core tasks doing something of very low cognitive complexity. Sometimes, being in the shower creates these sorts of moments, but exercise that allows the mind to freewheel is also highly supportive.

When faced with the need to write a complex document such as a proposal or indeed anything to which I need to give thought, I find it helpful to jot down a few bullet points and then go for a 30-minute run during which I do not think of anything in particular. On my return, the output seems to flow very readily and it feels as if my default mode network has done much of the heavy lifting in the background.

If exercise is not already a daily habit, use BJ Fogg's principles of starting with tiny steps in the first instance and working when motivation is highest. Also, to elevate the ease of doing it as far as possible, it sometimes helps to find ways of exercising at home. This is possible with exercise bikes or low-cost resistance bands.

Here are some tips for doing more exercise:

- Build exercise into your plan on at least a weekly basis.

- Identify pursuits that will allow your brain's default mode network to work unhindered for half an hour or so.

Part 10: Cultivate the virtuous habits of high performance

Action	When
• Plan a programme to optimise your diet, sleep and exercise patterns in support of your goals.	Now

For further resources go to www.headstartbook.com

Conclusion:
Head-start-to-finish

A resilient mindset ready to achieve your goals

This concludes our ten-point plan for helping you build a resilient mindset and achieve your goals.

We've seen that we often fail in pursuit of our goals because we become attached to negative beliefs that become self-limiting. For that reason, much of the help offered in this book has been about reframing some of those beliefs particularly where they are to do with what we feel might be pre-conditions for success such as talent, confidence or motivation. By thinking of these as outputs rather than inputs of a successful mindset, it becomes possible to cease worrying about them. Of course, the emotional part of our brain will continue to sound off about them – for good evolutionary reasons – but following the tips in this book, you should find this manageable.

Having reframed some of our beliefs, we then went about building a resilient mindset. Resilience in its most narrow sense is our ability to bounce back from adversity. But in the context of this book it is much more than that. It is the ability to seek new challenges and to go after them with zest and curiosity. Most important of all, it is the ease with which we can take ourselves outside our comfort zone. It also includes the ability to persist and to exert self-control in the face of distractions and the ever-present temptation to procrastinate.

Twentieth century prime minister Harold MacMillan was once asked what it was that prime ministers feared most. His response: 'Events, dear boy, events.' Whatever the nature of your goals, it is inevitable that you too will be confronted by forces in whatever form that will get in the way of achieving them. While you may not be able to exert much control over these events, what you can control is your emotional reaction to them. This book has given you a number of tools to help you limit a negative emotional reaction to adversity and to sustain focus on your goals.

Earlier, I wrote that success in goal pursuit relies on the interplay between our beliefs and behaviours. The figure below shows the journey that we have taken in this book as a diagram.

THE HEAD START PLAN

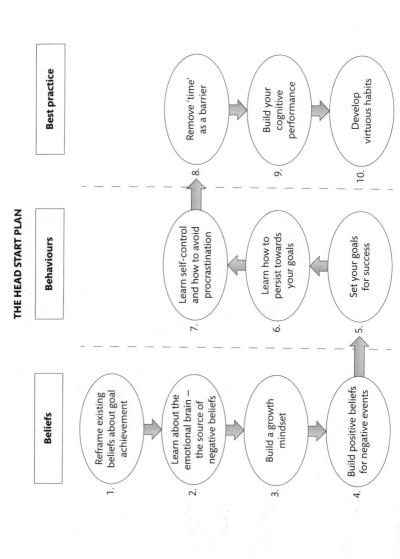

Beliefs	Behaviours	Best practice
1. Reframe existing beliefs about goal achievement	5. Set your goals for success	8. Remove 'time' as a barrier
2. Learn about the emotional brain – the source of negative beliefs	6. Learn how to persist towards your goals	9. Build your cognitive performance
3. Build a growth mindset	7. Learn self-control and how to avoid procrastination	10. Develop virtuous habits
4. Build positive beliefs for negative events		

Even with an optimal mindset, we are still required to get on and do what is needed to ultimately achieve our goals. Whatever your goals, your success will depend upon the choices you make each day whether confronted with an unexpected difficulty or the temptation to procrastinate when you know that you need to work on a process goal.

At these times, you will hear a voice inside your head (guess who?) telling you that you've timed out, that you're too tired or that it was simply not meant to be. At this point, review your action plan and get back in touch with your overarching purpose. Remind yourself how and why you got started towards your outcome goal. And remember the strategies in this book that were designed to help you persist and maximise your self-control.

Whatever ultimate success looks like, whatever the shape of your outcome goal, the best parting advice I can give you is to immerse yourself as far as possible in the process and, as odd as this may sound, learn to love it even when it doesn't feel as if things are going terribly well.

Many people that achieve remarkable success reflect that it was in some ways better to travel than to arrive. They often envy those at the outset of their own journeys with any number of battles and setbacks ahead of them. This is why it is uncommon to find successful entrepreneurs happily retiring to a tropical paradise and sitting on the beach. They are driven by the feeling of success at having built something and for all the sense of achievement they might be feeling and in spite of the likely attainment of financial independence, the likelihood is that they will start the process all over again.

This may sound bizarre from the standpoint of the beginning of your journey but consider the words of W Somerset Maugham about the character in a short story called 'Mayhew', whose life he describes as a success because: 'He did what he wanted, and he died when his goal was in sight and never knew the bitterness of an end achieved.'

So with an emphasis on the process in mind, in the Appendix of this book you will find a step-by-step summary of all the tasks that will help you along the way to your own success. So get your head together, take the first step... and enjoy the journey!

Appendix

Your Head Start plan summary

Part 1: Beliefs

Action	When
• If you haven't done so already, buy youself a journal in which to make notes as you work through this book. (or you may prefer to use your phone)	Now
• Read over the myths in this chapter. Make a note of your reaction to them. Write down any thoughts that come to mind. There is no need to judge your thoughts – just make a note of them.	Now
• Keep a diary for a week to capture your emotional chatter. Write down your thoughts in the raw language in which they pop into your head. Note at what or whom these thoughts are directed.	For the next week
• Put some distance between you and your emotional brain. As a negative thought pops into your head, play it back to yourself but first insert the words: 'The emotional part of my brain is saying that...'	From now on
• Start a news fast. Avoid watching or listening to broadcast news and reduce your exposure to other sources such as social media.	From now on

Action	When
• Read books such as *Do Humankind's Best Days Lie Ahead?* and *The Better Angels of Our Nature* by Stephen Pinker or *Non-Zero* by Robert Wright to promote your optimism about the world.	In the future
• Ask yourself where you have a fixed mindset, particularly when it comes to the ambitions or dreams that drew you to this book. Make a note in your journal of the fixed mindset beliefs that you currently hold.	Now
• Add to your diary any fixed mindset thoughts that pop into your head. Remember to capture the language in its raw state.	From now on
• Start to build a growth mindset plan: Who has achieved great things in this area that I can learn from? How can I get feedback in order to grow my abilities? Where can I find challenges to help me learn and hone my skills?	Now
• Find something that feels well outside your comfort zone and give it a go, even if it makes you feel vulnerable to do so. Look for a weekend course for beginners that offers a safe environment. Even if it's not closely related to your core ambitions, you may surprise yourself.	In the future
• Look out for the negativity bias and catch yourself hanging on to negative experiences. Make a note in your journal when this happens. This self-awareness is half the battle in dealing with setbacks.	From now on
• This is a repetition from an action on the previous page	From now on
• When you experience adversity, complete the perspective-talking exercise. Write down the worst-case outcome, the best-case outcome and then the most likely case.	From now on
• Use the Adversity worksheet when you experience adversity as a self-coaching tool to step through your explanatory style. Use evidence in your disputation.	From now on

Action	When
• When you experience adversity, talk through your completed Adversity worksheet with a trusted colleague or friend.	From now on
• Argue with your own pessimistic self-talk as if these negative thoughts were being shouted at you by a drunk in the street.	From now on
• Counter the negativity bias by writing a gratitude list at the beginning of each week.	Every Monday morning
• Accentuate the positive by keeping a success diary.	Daily

Part 2: Behaviours

Action	When
• Identify your outcome goal and move from saying to yourself 'I've always wanted to...' to 'My goal is to...'	Now
• Complete your mid-level goals.	Now
• Construct a goal-mapping sheet and pin it to your wall in your office or somewhere visible where you work.	Now
• Complete the process goals at the bottom of your goal-mapping sheet.	Now
• Find authoritative courses or tutors that have well-established methods of helping you build your abilities.	In the near future
• Look for ways of getting feedback on your efforts.	From now on
• Find ways to be taken out of your comfort zone.	In the future
• In your journal, keep an ear out for fixed mindset chatter and pessimistic explanatory style. If you hear these from your emotional brain, remember that grit is an output of a growth mindset combined with optimistic explanatory style.	From now on

Action	When
● Do the Grit test and make a note of the result.	Now
● Do the Grit test again and note any change.	One year from now
● Review your goal-mapping structure.	One year from now
● Identify your single 'marshmallows'.	Now
● Establish your purpose by completing your obituary exercise and sticking the results where you can see them.	Now
● Complete the mental contrasting exercise, visualising each of your process goals and then the marshmallow that may prevent you accomplishing them.	Now
● Write your 'If–then' strategies for dealing with each threat to your process goals.	Now
● Using BJ Fogg's model of behavioural change, plan your activity around those times when you believe your motivation will be highest.	Now
● Seek partners and buddies to collaborate on your goals and with whom you can form a social contract.	From now on
● Identify what existing routines can act as triggers that will most successfully prompt you to begin work on your process goals.	Now

Part 3: Best practice

Action	When
● Let go of the need to be busy.	From now on
● Identify the three big things you need to achieve in any given week.	Every Monday morning
● Eliminate multi-tasking as far as possible.	From now on
● Turn off all alerts on your devices for email and social media.	Now

Action	When
• Use the Pomodoro Technique in whatever form works for you.	Daily
• Use out-of-office or other filters when not in email.	From now on
• Be a time hawk and be ruthless with your time.	From now on
• Let go of 'timing out' as an excuse and tell yourself: 'I didn't run out of time. I chose to do something else.'	From now on
• Plan a daily ten-minute mindfulness session in your schedule, ideally first thing in the morning.	Daily
• Make a note in your journal of your experience, noting what thoughts might be distracting you from focus on the breath.	Daily
• Make a note of any general changes in your temperament or behaviour as a result of your mindfulness practice.	From now on
• Plan a programme to optimise your diet, sleep and exercise patterns in support of your goals.	Now

Notes

1) 'British success at the Olympics is not just a national achievement', *The Daily Telegraph*, 15 August 2016 http://www.telegraph.co.uk/business/2016/08/15/british-success-at-the-olympics-is-not-just-a-national-achieveme/

2) BBC Radio Four's *World at One*, 16 August 2016

3) Carney, Dana R, Cuddy, Amy JC &Yap, Andy J, 'Power Posing. Brief Nonverbal Displays Affect Neuroendocrine Levels and Risk Tolerance', *Psychological Science*, **21** (10), 2010

4) Pinker, Steven, *Do Humankind's Best Days Lie Ahead? The Munk Debates*, House of Anansi Press, 2016

5) Dweck, Carol, *Mindset: The New Psychology of Success*, Robinson, 2006

6) Ericsson, Anders & Pool, Robert, *Peak: Secrets from the New Science of Expertise*, Bodley Head, 2016

7) Maguire, EA, et al, 'Navigation-related structural change in the hippocampi of taxi drivers', *Proceedings of the National Academy of Sciences of the United States of America* **97** (8), 2000

8) Briceno, Eduardo, The Power of Belief – Mindset and Success, ted.com https://ed.ted.com/on/aVMPCOpr

9) Grant, Adam & Sandberg, Sheryl, *Option B: Facing Adversity, Building Resilience, and Finding Joy*, W H Allen, 2017

10) Tedeschi, Richard, & Calhoun, Lawrence, 'Posttraumatic Growth: Conceptual Foundations and Empirical Evidence', *Psychological Inquiry*, **15** (1), 2004

11) Murray, Andy, *Seventy-Seven: My Road to Wimbledon Glory*, Headline, 2013

12) 'Andy will be hoping his Castorri has a fairytale ending', *The Daily Mail*, 6 July 2013 http://www.dailymail.co.uk/sport/tennis/article-2357588/Wimbledon-2013-Andy-Murray-reliant-psychologist-Alexis-Castorri.html

13) 'The Neurotic Zen of Larry David', *Rolling Stone*, 6 July 2011 https://www.rollingstone.com/music/features/the-neurotic-zen-of-larry-david-20110804

14) Eagleman, David, *Incognito: The Secret Lives of the Brain*, Pantheon Books, 2011

15) 'Roger Federer reveals the secrets behind his incredible success', *The Daily Telegraph*, 7 November 2014 http://www.telegraph.co.uk/sport/tennis/rogerfederer/11216129/Roger-Federer-reveals-the-secrets-behind-his-incredible-success.html

16) Lewis, Michael, *Moneyball: The Art of Winning an Unfair Game*, WW Norton, 2004

17) Seligman, Martin, *Learned Optimism*, Alfred A Knopf, 1990

18) Seligman, ibid

19) Collins, Jim & Porras, Jerry, *Built to Last: Successful Habits of Visionary Companies*, HarperCollins, 1994

20) Lee Duckworth, Angela, *Grit: Why Passion and Resilience are the Secrets to Success*, Vermillion, 2017

21) Ericsson, ibid

22) Higgins, George V, *On Writing: Advice for Those Who Write to Publish (or Would Like to)*, Holt & Co, 1991

23) Peters, Steve, Optimising the Performance of the Human Mind, TEDxYouth@Manchester, 2012 https://www.youtube.com/watch?v=R-KI1D5NPJs

24) Chagnon, Napoleon, *Noble Savages: My Life Among Two Dangerous Tribes – The Yanomamö and the Anthropologists*, Simon & Schuster, 2014

25) Duckworth, ibid

26) Duckworth, ibid

27) Mischel, Walter, *The Marshmallow Test: Understanding Self-Control and How to Master It*, Corgi, 2015

28) Mischel, ibid

29) Owen, Mark, *No Easy Day*, Dutton Books, 2012

30) Fogg, BJ, Website: www.bjfogg.com/

31) Eyal, Nir, 'Have We Been Thinking About Willpower the Wrong Way for 30 Years?', *Harvard Business Review*, 23 November 2016

32) Inzlicht, Michael, Website: http://michaelinzlicht.com/research/

33) Itzler, Jesse, *Living with a SEAL: 31 Days Training with the Toughest Man on the Planet*, Center Street, 2017

34) Goleman, Daniel, 'Leadership That Gets Results', *Harvard Business Review*, March/April 2000

35) Nass, Clifford, 'How Multi-tasking is Affecting the Way You Think', Stanford Alumni video, 3 October 2013 https://www.youtube.com/watch?v=MPHJMIOwKjE

36) Greenfield, Susan, *ID: The Quest for Meaning in the 21st Century*, Sceptre, 2009

37) Hanson, Rick & Mendius, Richard, *Buddha's Brain: The Practical Neuroscience of Happiness, Love and Wisdom*, New Harbinger, 2009

38) Hanson & Mendius, ibid

39) Czeisler, Charles, 'Sleep Deficit: The Performance Killer', *Harvard Business Review*, October 2006

40) Asprey, Dave, *Head Strong*, Harper Wave, 2017

Index